Legislative Study No. 31

THE ROLE OF LEGISLATION IN LAND USE PLANNING FOR DEVELOPING COUNTRIES

by
Gregory K. Wilkinson
Chief, Land and Water Legislation Section
Legislation Branch, Legal Office

FOOD AND AGRICULTURE ORGANIZATION OF THE UNITED NATIONS
Rome, 1985

The designations employed and the presentation of material in this publication do not imply the expression of any opinion whatsoever on the part of the Food and Agriculture Organization of the United Nations concerning the legal status of any country, territory, city or area or of its authorities, or concerning the delimitation of its frontiers or boundaries.

M-59
ISBN 92-5-101465-5

CONTENTS

Page

FOREWORD

Productive land resources are an increasingly scarce commodity in many developing countries. Thus, as desertification, pollution and urbanization continue their advance during the second half of the Twentieth Century, rational planning of the use of land has become imperative for economic and social development and -- in some cases -- for survival.

Fortunately, the scarcity of productive land resources has generated an increasing awareness in many developing countries that existing mechanisms for allocating rural lands to different uses are not working. Thus, there has been an upsurge in demand for assistance in the preparation of land use plans and the upgrading of local planning infrastructure and personnel. At FAO this need for help has resulted in a significant increase in land use related technical assistance. It has also stimulated an evaluation of the process of land use planning and a re thinking of the role of various technical disciplines in that process.

One of the disciplines which has had its role enhanced through this evaluation of land use planning is the law. At the technical level within FAO, carefully drafted legislation is increasingly viewed as an essential element of a rational land use planning process. Thus, for instance, a recent conference of planning experts was convened at FAO's Rome Headquarters to advise on proposed land use planning guidelines prepared by an Interdepartmental Working Group on Land Use Planning created by the Director General in 1983. In its commentary on the proposed Guidelines, this expert group *inter alia* declared that, as part of an effort to introduce rationality into the process of land use planning in developing countries,

> "Appropriate legislation should be developed for the purpose of providing clearly stated land use policies and objectives; creating suitable land use planning institutions; requiring the use of sound planning procedures and techniques; promoting the development of a consensus about land use and encouraging a practical monitoring and enforcement mechanism..."

The present study, by the Chief of the Agrarian and Water Law Section of the FAO Legislation Branch, is intended to explore in greater depth the value of legislation to the land use planning process. It is, on the one hand, an exploration of the ways in which legislation serves to provide the structural underpinnings for and connections between the technical disciplines which have long been associated with the land use planning effort. It is also intended as a practical guide for lawyers or planners who may be faced with the task of framing or implementing land use legislation and who thus require a solid understanding of the disciplines of law and planning and how they are related. It is our hope that the reader will find the study more than sufficient to meet both of these purposes.

Finally, inasmuch as this study relies to a considerable extent upon existing national legislation to serve as examples of many of the points which are made, it is recognized that minor corrections or modifications may be required to take account of any changes in the legislation itself. The Legislaton Branch will accordingly be grateful to those who point out the need for such corrections or necessary modifications so that they may be taken into account in any future edition.

Francis M. Mifsud
Chief, Legislation Branch
Legal Office

INTRODUCTION

Land is the most basic natural resource available for the social and economic development of people. Together with water, it combines to produce other valuable resources including topsoil, forests, pasture, wildlife habitat and even fisheries. In turn, these resources allow for specific uses to be made of land, including crop production, pasturage, timber harvesting, mining residential or commercial development, waste disposal and recreation, among others. Through the forces of nature - or the prior actions of human beings - the productive land resources which support such uses appear in differing measures of abundance in different geographic areas. The distribution of resources, however, is by no means static; by their actions, people have the capability of altering the mix. They can act to conserve or deplete existing productive resources or they can take the steps necessary to increase certain resources, either by increasing the stock of that resource or by improving the accessibility of the resource to potential users.

If the location and abundance of productive land resources are not static, neither are decisions concerning the use of such resources made in a vacuum. By acting to increase or deplete one land-related resource, people may well have an effect upon other resources. Indeed, it is not unreasonable to view potential (or existing) land uses in terms of their compatibility or non-compatibility with other uses. Thus, for example, increasing the amount of land devoted to irrigated or rainfed agriculture may decrease forestry or pasture resources or wildlife habitat if existing forest lands are cleared or if pasture and habitat are destroyed in order that farming may be expanded. The same decision may also yield impacts such as an alteration of traditional land ownership patterns or a disruption or termination of the seasonal migration routes of nomadic peoples or wildlife. In short, not only do land use patterns fail to stand still, but some land use decisions may be essentially compatible with other important existing or proposed uses of land, while other land use decisions are not.

Given the complexities of land use decision-making and the inter-relationship of the process with other aspects of mankind's effort to lead a socially and economically rewarding life, it seems self-evident that rational land-use decision making should be encouraged and ad hoc, ill-considered decision making avoided. To this end, for example, the recently adopted FAO World Soil Charter sets forth as one of its Guidelines for Action, the incorporation of principles of rational land use and management into appropriate resource legislation [1/]. Unfortunately, as with many self-evident truths, practice often diverges considerably from theory, with ad hoc land use decision-making constituting the norm and reasoned, considered decision-making the exception in many jurisdictions.

The consequences of an ad hoc approach to land-use decision making, however, loom large when a few demographic facts are taken into account. Currently about seventy-five million persons are added yearly to the world's population, with annual increases of 100 million expected by the year 2000 [2/]. By the year 2025, the world's population may approach eight billion, a figure approximately double the present level [3/]. Even the six billion people who are expected to inhabit the planet in the year 2000 will require an agricultural output some 50 to 60 percent greater than in 1980 [4/]. Further, as world population soars, pressures on agricultural land mount, due to problems of soil erosion and degradation and to the conversion of agricultural land to other uses. Indeed, long-term soil loss and soil degradation may be occuring on one-third of the agricultural land in the world, while the problem of conversion is nearly universal [5/]. In short, land is being pressured by a variety of forces and, unless intelligent decisions are made, something other than optimum patterns of land use will likely result.

1/ FAO, World Soil Charter, 1982, p. 3.

2/ Arts and Church, Soil Erosion - The Next Crisis, Wisc. L.R. 1982, p. 559.

3/ See C. McEvedy and R. Jones, Atlas of World Population History, p. 350.

4/ FAO, Agriculture : Towards 2000, 1981.

5/ Arts and Church, supra, p. 559.

The conclusion just recited is disarmingly simple to state and hints at the intuitively obvious : rational, intelligent and informed land-use decisions will produce superior utilization of limited resources with better economic and social results. This facile conclusion raises, however, the equally obvious question of just how do you generate rational, intelligent and informed land-use decisions ? Moreover, even if you generate such decisions, how do you convince anybody else - particularly those who make their own decisions everyday in the fields, the forests, the grazing areas - to follow them ? Both are fair questions and it is by confronting them that we arrive at the purpose of this study.

The author is a lawyer not formally trained in the sciences of soil classification, engineering or sociology. He and his colleagues in the Agrarian and Water Section of the FAO Legislation Branch are asked with increasing frequency, however, to deal with these sciences and the people who practice them in order to provide the legal support for rural land use planning systems that will generate rational, intelligent and informed land-use decisions in developing countries. In pursuing this task, they have had to contend with several facts that have influenced the approach to the subject of land use decision-making.

First, they - we - [6/] have found that relatively little scholarly discourse or actual legislative drafting has occurred on the subject of rural land development law in developing countries; or that if it exists,

---

6/ Although this work has been written by the Chief of the Agrarian and Legislation Section of the FAO Legislation Branch, the views expressed frequently are shared by colleagues in the Branch. Moreover, many of the experiences related herein have been common ones; thus, the occasional use in this work of the first person plural "we". Certainly in spirit - if not in precise form - this work represents a shared perspective on land development legislation in the developing world.

it is not readily discoverable for people like us who are being called upon to actually draft rural land-use development laws. This dearth of prior effort contrasts markedly with the wealth of legally-related material on the subject of urban land-use legislation or even rural land-use legislation in developed countries. Nevertheless, the relative lack of prior activity in the field has produced its own benefit. While it has perhaps slowed our preparation of a "model law" suitable for all occasions, it has also required us to do our own basic research and to think conceptually about the purpose, the place and the form of rural land-use legislation in a developing country. The benefit generated by this is that our thought processes have not been confined to furrows previously plowed. Indeed, the necessity of considering the problem without much prior legal guidance has allowed us to perhaps break some new ground. The risk of such an approach, of course, is that by not being aware of the mistakes of others, we condemn ourselves to repeating them. We recognize this risk, and to minimize its occurrence, have sought and obtained the guidance of technical personnel in a variety of fields. Most helpful in this regard, has been the FAO Inter-Departmental Working Group on Land Use Planning, established by the FAO Director-General in 1983 for the purpose of bringing an interdisciplinary approach to rural land-use planning.

A second basic fact encountered in the course of our work is that the law and lawyers do not exactly leap to mind when the subject of rural land-use is raised. Often they are not thought of at all, with the emphasis given instead to data collection, cadastral surveys, map-making and the like. When they are thought of, lawyers sometimes are perceived as nuisances who simply get in the way of - and thus impede - the really important technical work required to produce a rural land use development plan.

It is not the purpose of this work to argue the merits of law and lawyers versus scientific, sociological and economic data collection and evaluation. Obviously, rational, intelligent and informed land use decisions are unlikely to be made where the extent of available resources, the nature of land-related problems and the economic and sociological impact of land-use decisions are unknown. Just as obviously, however, we believe it is inappropriate to view the law and the technical disciplines associated with land development as unrelated. Similarly, it is inaccurate to see lawyers and the practitioners of the scientific disciplines concerned with land-use planning, as competitors. From our work, we believe that the law and lawyers - if properly cognizant of their role - can play an essential part in the land-use process by, inter alia drafting the legislation which creates a land-use decision-making infrastructure appropriate to the size and sophistication of the country at hand and which guides and promotes the workings of that infrastructure through the establishment of policies and guidelines, the specification of procedures, the establishment of provisions for public participation and the creation of implementation and enforcement powers. In short, rather than viewing the law and lawyers as antithetical to the land-use decision-making process, we view them as compatible and complementary.

Thus, our purpose in writing this study is at least two-fold. On the one hand, we hope that by analyzing land-use development legislation and its constituent elements we will provide a reference for others who, like ourselves may have to contend with either the drafting or implementation of such legislation. Inquiring about the elements of rural land use legislation, discussing the nature of the infrastructure which might provide the best decision-making mechanism, and analyzing the factors that ought to be considered by such an infrastructure, we hope, will permit some conclusions about the larger question of what makes a workable land-use law. If we have done our job adequately, it may eliminate the need to figuratively re-invent the wheel each time an effort is undertaken to develop land-use legislation in a new setting.

On the other hand, we also intend by this study to advocate the importance of law and lawyers in the land use decision-making process. In our view, the law has the ability to tie widely disparate scientific, economic and social elements together into a coherent whole. It can provide the structure for using the data collected and analyzed by other disciplines, in order to make decisions. It can provide the standards against which those decisions shall be adjudged and it can compel the consideration of factors which the advocates of a particular development project might prefer to ignore. In short, legislation, has an important role to play in the rural land development process: it provides the structural framework and the legal controls for rational, intelligent and informed land-use decision-making; it serves as well as the linkage to connect the different substantive disciplines that make up the planning process.

Thus, during the course of writing this work, we have found ourselves engaged in a process of discussing law to one potential audience -- the planners -- and planning to another audience; viz., the lawyers. Given the historical lack of intersection between these two disciplines such a bridge may be viewed as having some utility.

Finally, though, we are experienced enough to know that sophistry cannot replace substance in the crucible. In other words, whether we convince planners of the importance of the role of lawyers in the rural land use decision-making process or lawyers of the importance of understanding the basics of rural development planning depends far more on the substance of our arguments rather than how we argue. Further, it should be understood that this study is not intended as the last word on rural land-use development law in developing countries; a first word would be considerably more accurate. If it provokes as many questions as it answers in the course of thoughtful discussion, our sense of purpose will have been satisfied. With these caveats in mind, we turn to an analysis of rural land-use legislation in developing countries.

CHAPTER I - OVERVIEW

The precise recipe for rational, informed land-use decision-making in the rural sector of developing countries is likely to elude discovery for the foreseeable future. Unfortunately, however, neither the pressure of development nor the need for wise decision-making are likely to abate pending that discovery. Hence, notwithstanding the lack of precision involved, it is a useful effort to attempt to identify and analyze the factors that encourage - and perhaps even occasionally result in - intelligent land-use decisions. The effort is especially warranted in the legislative area in view of the increasing awareness in developing countries that legislation has a role in the land-use decision-making process. Already this awareness is being felt in the form of requests for assistance by lawyers who face, with more and more frequency, the task of developing a legislative scheme that will yield wise land-use decisions.

It is useful to begin this study with a general overview of the factors that appear to be involved in planned - as opposed to *ad hoc* - land use decision-making. For this purpose, certain definitions recently adopted by the FAO Inter-Departmental Working Group (IDWG) on Land Use Planning, serve as a helpful point of departure. The IDWG has been charged with the responsibility of formulating a coherent, inter-disciplinary approach to FAO land-use planning projects and, as part of its duties, has developed agreed upon definitions of "land", "land use", "planning" and "land use planning". Of these, the definitions of "land use" and "land use planning" are especially pertinent.

"Land use" has been defined by the IDWG as "the function of the land determined by natural conditions and human intervention" [7/]. In other words

---

7/ The IDWG goes on to state with reference to "land use" :

> "It is useful to categorize land use according to status and employment of the land; for example, crop land, forest land, grazing land, nature reserve, aquaculture, non-agricultural land, etc. and multipurpose uses."

The Working Group then adds,

> "It is necessary to distinguish present land use (the way in which land is used at present) and potential land use (how it could be used with or without improvements)."

land use is a non-judgemental result. It is simply the situation which results from decisions made by man or nature without regard to whether those decisions are wise, informed, planned or <u>ad hoc</u>.

"Land use planning" on the other hand is defined in a way which clearly shows it to be a means to a desired end :

> "Land use planning is the process of evaluating land and alternative patterns of land use and other physical, social and economic conditions for the purpose of selecting and adopting the kinds of land use and courses of action best calculated to achieve specified objectives." [8/].

8/ The IDWG on Land Use Planning elaborates considerably on its definition of land use planning by adding the following :

> "Land use planning may be at national, regional or village level. The process ideally involves the participation of the land users. It entails bringing together a wide array of data : physical, technological, economic and institutional, and integrating them systematically for the purpose of developing a workable plan and programme of action. Interactions between land uses within an area, or in the neighbouring regions, must be taken into account.
>
> "The programme or plan may be subject to institutional or other constraints such as land tenure systems, customs, and taboos. However, in the long run, these institutions are subject to changes to facilitate better land use. Nevertheless it should be recognized that the programme or plan must, at best, be regarded as an ideal and that in an economy undergoing profound structural changes, the desired optimum patterns of land use may not be obtainable in a practical sense. The programme or plan will change according to the wants and preferences of consumers, changes in the land, advances in technology, and variations in the level and distribution of income. The essential task is to indicate those patterns of use which are superior to the present or alternative land uses, in terms both of spatial allocation of land among different uses and the intensity of land use, which together determine the patterns of land use."

When viewed in pari materia with the definition of land use, it can be seen that land use planning is the mechanism by which judgment can be injected into a previously non-judgemental situation. Stated differently, it is the means by which the term "land use" can be made more "rational".

It is instructive to examine the IDWG's definition of "land use planning" for the purpose of identifying its constituent parts. When this is done, it is seen that the definition is composed of the following distinct elements :

1. specified objectives;
2. appraisal of land and alternative patterns of land use;
3. assessment of other physical, social and economic conditions;
4. a process of calculation and selection; and
5. a process of adoption.

This study views these elements not only as parts of an abstract definition; it also sees them as crucial constituents of any legislation which seeks to provide a practical, workable legal structure designed to produce intelligent land use decisions. Over the course of the next few paragraphs we shall outline these elements - and several others - more fully. In the remaining chapters of this work we shall analyze each such element in more detail not only for the purpose of discussing its individual component parts, but also to demonstrate why any effort to draft rural land-use legislation should at least weigh the importance of the identified elements, even if one or more are ultimately excluded in the course of actual drafting.

1. Policies and Priorities Regarding Rural Land-Use

As the FAO land use planning group has determined, rational land use decision-making is a process directed at the achievement of "specified objectives". These objectives, we believe, can appropriately be described as rural land development policies and priorities. Typically, they are determined by the central government; they may, however, be developed in the first instance at the regional or even the local governmental level. In a general way, they determine the direction of the land use decision-making process and serve also as standards for assessing whether a particular land-use decision is compatible with the public interest. Without such guideposts, a systematic approach to rural land development is unlikely to develop. Instead, land-use decisions are more likely to be made on an ad hoc basis that will be less likely to consider the public interest, less likely to consider development alternatives and less likely to balance project benefits against societal costs.

For the purpose of drafting land use legislation, we believe it is important to consider whether there is, or should be, government policy on a variety of issues. Such issues include, inter alia social concerns, the preservation of prime agricultural land, revenue policy and land development, the control of agricultural impacts on other uses, compulsory tilling and control of erosion. They should include as well, policies about indigenous populations and protection of the environment. In Chapter II of this work, we shall explore the importance of these issues and others to the legislative drafting process.

Further, as we discuss in Chapter II, government priorities related directly or indirectly to land may also serve as guideposts for intelligent decision-making. The priorities which are considered especially important, and hence are discussed in more depth in the course of this study include inter alia, export versus staple crop preferences; water development priorities; agricultural versus urban development priorities; and agricultural versus forestry priorities.

2. Existing Land Use Decision-Making Structure

In addition to understanding government policies and priorities concerning land use, knowledge of the operation of existing land-use decision-making mechanisms, whether governmental or non-governmental, is crucial. Regarding the government, it is important to understand what institutions are involved and at what level. Does the administrative process (assuming one exists) operate by consensus or by fiat ? Are there vertical connections among different levels of administration ? Do horizontal connections exist which promote an interdisciplinary approach on any one level? Also important to know is the extent to which the views of special interest groups are considered in the formal decision-making process and whether the decisions which are reached are subject to independent review.

3. Customary Practices

At the non-governmental level, it is important to understand the customary practices which exert influence on the decision-making process. In a very practical way customs concerning marriage, dissolution, inheritance and wealth accumulation may be more determinative of land use patterns and practices than proclamations issuing from a ministry exercising nominal jurisdiction over land from a capital city located hundreds of kilometers away. Similarly, the seasonal migration of workers, the movement of animals or a relatively aged or young population may suggest certain land use decisions and not others. Legislation which considers these patterns and practices is likely to be more practical and more respected (even, perhaps, if it is contrary to a particular pattern or practice) than land-use legislation written in ignorance of social customs, historical and economic practices or demography. Indeed, in its comments to the definition of "land use planning", the aforementioned Inter-Departmental Working Group expressly recognized that a programme of land use could be subject to such constraints as "customs and taboos". Obviously legislation which recognizes such constraints and attempts to deal with them intelligently, is likely to be more influential.

4. Land Ownership Patterns and Policies

For similar reasons, there should be an understanding of the nature of land ownership and occupancy patterns. Legislation which restricts or promotes development on government owned land may have social and economic consequences entirely different from those that result from legislation affecting land that is privately owned. Similarly, a land use decision impacting land that is densely populated may have greater social, economic and political consequences than one which affects scarcely populated land.

Moreover, the government may have specific policies related to land ownership (land to the tiller or restraints on alienation, for example) which, if ignored, could render land-use legislation less effective. Finally, legislation which fails to provide security to private owners through an effective registration system or other means, may have difficulty inducing those owners to participate in or abide by the results of the land use decision-making process.

5. Land Resource Inventory

Apart from a knowledge of existing customs, institutions and land ownership patterns, intelligent land-use decision making requires a thorough knowledge of rural land and related natural resources. Indeed, it is difficult to understand how intelligent land use decisions can be made in the absence of knowledge about the quality and geographic distribution of soils, the quality, location and availability of water resources and the distribution of forests, habitat and grazing lands, among other things. For the legislative drafter, in fact, the issue is not likely to be whether appropriate land-use legislation should provide for a land resource inventory; almost certainly it should. Instead, the issues may involve the detail (and thus the time and expense) required for such an inventory, the responsibility for its preparation (i.e., whether at the national, regional or local level or some combination thereof); and the extent of its coverage (i.e., whether, for example, it should attempt to cover the entire country or instead should be targeted at smaller areas facing particularly acute development pressure). These issues are discussed in more detail in Chapter V of this work.

6. Land Use Decision-Making Process

As noted previously, the FAO land use working group views decision-making about land as a "process". That view is certainly appropriate in connection with the drafting of land use legislation. To a considerable degree such legislation should be concerned with the process of developing a consensus about land use so as to achieve desired results that are consistent with agreed upon principles. We explain.

A. Development of a Consensus

A recurrent problem encountered in many developing countries is that government pronouncements sometimes have little force and effect beyond the walls of the ministry from whence they issue. Perhaps this results from the isolation of the policy maker; perhaps it results from the lack of any stake in the government's plans on the part of persons subject to the pronouncement. Whatever the reason, poor infrastructure and typically weak enforcement mechanisms often multiply the government's difficulties in overcoming indifference or outright hostility, with the result that the government's plans and pronouncements go unheeded.

Alteration of the foregoing situation may well require basic changes in the process by which land use decisions are made. More specifically, it appears to require a sharing of decision-making power between professional planning administrators and those who are expected to abide by the decisions which are made *viz.*, the rural inhabitants whose farming, forestry,grazing and other agrarian activities may be impacted. Undoubtedly, such a shared, or "consensus" approach to land use decision-making is more difficult to effectuate than a planning approach which consists of unilateral decision-making following the sifting of technical data in the relatively rarified atmosphere of a planning ministry. At a minimum the process requires a more consistent and extensive liaison between the government and the governed; wide-spread training in the basis of land use decision-making; and a willingness to open the decision-making process to non-professional, non-governmental participants if it is to be more than just an academic exercise that will be ignored when the time arises to put such decisions into actual practice.

For the lawyer, the challenge is to design a law which overcomes the normally insular nature of land-use decision-making and establishes a linkage between government planning administrators and the people affected by planning decisions, thus promoting a two-way flow of information between planners and affected individuals. At the same time, the lawyer must be careful not to encourage the decision-making mechanism to degenerate into a situation which promotes discussion and negotiation as the end rather than the means of the process. As noted above, it is important that the process remain directed at the achievement of desired results. Thus, there must be a legal structure which is not only sufficiently open to produce a more participatory approach to decision-making; the structure must also assure that the process continues to move toward the goal of a land-use decision. Our thoughts on how this might be accomplished are contained in Chapter VI, *infra*.

B. Land Use Principles

For the purpose of guiding the process as it moves to a decision - and also for the purpose of evaluating any such decision in terms of its consistency with the public interest - it is also imperative to establish certain principles which serve to generally guide and control the process. While of course these principles (like the workings of the process itself) may vary according to the specific circumstances involved in each country, it is useful to provide that the land use decision-making process as well as the decisions which it produces, comport with several basic rules related to the recommendation of a particular land use from among several alternatives. Given that cost-benefit analysis (CBA) is frequently the principle tool used by decision-makers for the purpose of making such selections, we have developed several recommended statutory guidelines designed to broaden the focus of CBA and thus, improve its utility as a means of making rational choices about land use. These recommended guidelines are also discussed in Chapter VI, infra.

7. Implementation of Plans

Notwithstanding the utilization of a consensus approach, land use decision making is not land use implementation. For the land use control process to move beyond the paper exercise stage there must exist the means of actually implementing decisions which are made. A variety of implementation measures present themselves, however, and it is important to understand their benefits and deficiencies. In this study, for purposes of discussion, we have categorized implementation measures into two broad groups : legal and extra-legal.

Legal implementation measures are those generally exercised in strict accordance with statutory provisions that carefully outline the extent of the measure, describe the manner of its exercise and provide review procedures to forestall its abuse. One such measure is the exercise of regulatory power - itself a classification which describes a variety of specific powers including: 1) the issuance or denial of building and development permits; 2) zoning classifications; 3) the assertion of public trust authority; and 4) nuisance controls, among others. Similarly, exercise of the eminent domain power is a legal implementation measure that raises a host of sub-issues including questions of taking versus regulation; taking versus planning and just compensation among others. Finally, the taxing power may be considered an implementation measure of a legal character when it is exercised in the form of preferential assessments, restraints on tax-financed investments (such as conversion restrictions on preferentially assessed agricultural land) and investment tax concessions.

Extra-legal implementation measures, on the other hand, are those land-use oriented programmes which - while typically possessing a basis in law - are not so strictly controlled by statute. Examples of non-legal measures would include the provision of agricultural extension services, rural oriented training programmes, rural research efforts and government promotion of particular land uses through price supports or other subsidies.

Chapter VII of this study describes in greater detail the various legal and non-legal measures just mentioned. It also attempts to point out the strength of each such measure and its weaknesses. This study does not, however, attempt to rank the various implementaton measures in terms of desireability nor does it attempt to provide a menu of an optimum mix of legal and non-legal approaches to implementation. Those are issues whose resolution depends upon the particular circumstances at hand. They thus are beyond the scope of this more general (and thus limited) exercise.

8. Enforcement and Modification of Land Use Development Plans

Apart from the means of implementation, there should also exist the means of enforcing the land use policy decisions which are reached. Unless the persons developing land (whether those "persons" are the government or the private sector) are required to comply with the determinations of land use policy makers, those policy determinations will be difficult to implement. Thus, whether the land developer is the government or a private person, he should be held to a standard of consistency with land use policies.

Coincidentally there should exist a practical means of reviewing development activities as well as a means of enforcing development policies and plans in the event of incompatible development efforts. In connection with individual, small-scale enterprises, this may mean locally administered, informal monitoring and local arbitration or penalty assessment. With more sophisticated projects, the enforcement controls may extend not only to a permit system but also to financial controls which might prohibit the government from funding directly or indirectly a project not consistent with previously determined development plans or policies. In all cases, as we explain in more detail *infra*, it is anticipated that the development of a consensus will be important to any enforcement effort.

In addition to the matter of enforcement, it is important to consider the question of plan modification. Because any plan is likely to be subject to influences that will necessitate changes over time, there should exist the means of periodically reviewing previously adopted land use plans and making changes to them. Moreover, as was the case with development of the original plans themselves, there should exist guidelines against which the changes may be evaluated and the means with which to develop a consensus about any proposed change.

9. Financing Land Use Development

Closely related to the implementation of land use decisions is the question of the financing of land use development. The question is a multidimensional one that presents a variety of sub-issues.

Viewed from the domestic perspective, financing directly involves the issue of revenue sources - and through the allocation of revenues, a determination of who controls development. If, for example, the national policy is to decentralize government decision making, land use decisions ostensibly may be a matter for regional, and even local, policy makers. But if revenue sources are not decentralized, *i.e.*, if the central government retains control over the main sources of government revenue, actual control over development, at best, is ambiguous. Even if the central government awards loans or grants to the regional or local decision-makers, it may in fact retain control through the imposition of conditions. If, on the other hand, it fails to provide revenues or permit regional or local decision-makers to develop their own revenue sources, it may effectively bar regional and local participation in the process of planning and implementing (and controlling) rural development. Financing, in short, can be a means of confirming - or rearranging - decision making or implementation authority otherwise allocated by law.

Viewed from the international perspective, financing has an equally large impact upon development control. The Central Government's Ministry of Finance, for example, may have only a minimal voice in the development of land use plans or the formulation of specific projects whose implementation is desired by other departments or other levels of government. If, however, the Ministry is the department of government designated to arrange national or international funding for rural development and if the Ministry operates autonomously in pursuing its task, actual control over development may in fact lie with the Finance Minister rather than with the ministries intended by rural development statutes to exercise such control.

Further, and apart from the matter of *de facto* control over development, unless thought is given to such issues as repatriation of profits concessions, tax holidays and the question of transfer of technology, the economic and social benefits otherwise obtainable by development could be lost in the scramble for outside investment. We discuss these additional matters in Chapter IX, *infra*.

10. Land Use Decision-Making Structure (Institutions and Administration)

Finally, of course, land use legislation must consider the question of the appropriate decision-making structure. We have saved such discussion for last, in part because it is an issue that should be approached only after many of the policy-related questions discussed above have been answered. In part too, the question of a decision-making structure is the most difficult to discuss in the abstract. What is "appropriate" really means what is appropriate in the specific circumstances at hand. Specific circumstances are almost infinite in their variety, however, and it is not really possible, in our view, to create the model land use decision-making structure suitable for all occasions. Any effort to do so - if too specific - would undoubtedly fail to take into account many of the particular, and important, problems faced in the real-world case at hand. Similarly, any effort to draft a broad proposal would almost certainly be too general if applied literally.

The final chapter of this work should not be read as a contradiction of the views just expressed. In it, we have admittedly attempted to set forth on paper one example of a proposed land-use planning structure. It must be stressed, however, that the system described therein is simply an example that is intended to further the (hopefully) provocative character of this work. If it causes the reader's own creative juices to flow; indeed, even if it simply provokes the reader's belief that he or she can do better, then it will have served its purpose. If, on the other hand, it is viewed uncritically and followed slavishly, it will have been abused. Considering the relative infancy of the field of rural land use legislation in developing countries, uncritical devotees are not especially useful - particularly to their clients.

We turn now to a more detailed analysis of the ideas which have been briefly presented hereinabove.

CHAPTER II - POLICIES AND PRIORITIES CONCERNING RURAL LAND USE

The process of rural land use planning, including the drafting and implementation of legislation, serves as a means to an end. It is a way by which disparate rural land uses can be more effectively ordered to achieve desired governmental policies and priorities. The direction of the land-use process is determined by these policies and priorities which, in turn, serve as general guidelines for determining whether a land use decision is consistent with the public interest as it has been formulated by the government. Understanding the nature of the government's policies and priorities respecting rural land use is thus imperative for the lawyer or planner faced with the drafting or implementation of rural land use legislation.

Finding the government's policies and priorities concerning rural land use development, unfortunately, is often difficult. Occasionally policies and priorirites may be clearly written and applied in formulating development decisions. More likely, however, such policies as exist are scattered throughout a variety of laws or are found, in the *de facto* workings of government ministries whose mandates yield varying degrees of contact with the land use process. Frequently too, an important policy exists in the mind of a single minister, and may change with his departure or even his attitude [9/]. Inter-ministerial or even inter-departmental coordination on matters of land use policy may, in turn, depend less on the manifest benefits of cooperation, than on the informal agreements - or indeed, the state of mind - of involved personnel.

9/ The fact that such "personalized" policy formulation exists should not cause the lawyer or planner to conclude that the situation is hopeless and give up. It may suggest simply that the task should include the devising of a mechanism which will tend to "de-personalize" the process by rendering the personal attitudes of an individual or single group less significant.

The fact that government policies and priorities may be difficult to track down, however, does not lessen the importance of attempting to determine them. For either the lawyer or the planner, it is a waste of time, effort and someone's money, to draft rural land use legislation that bears little or no relationship to the policies and priorities which the government seeks to implement. Indeed, land use planning, no matter how nicely laid out and ordered by statute, is arguably rational only to the extent that it efficiently and equitably serves the government's goals. In short, because land use planning is a means to an end, its worth may be measured to a not-inconsiderable extent by its success in achieving that end.

Woven throughout the foregoing paragraphs is the belief that the wise individual must search beyond the books - including this one - to determine the policies and priorities which legislation on rural land use development should seek to implement. To facilitate that search, however, we believe it is useful to examine in this work the kinds of policies and priorities which rural land use legislation might seek to achieve. While the discussion which follows makes no pretense of covering the universe of potential policies which may exist, we believe it to be sufficiently comprehensive to enable the lawyer or planner to frame intelligent questions and avoid overlooking any obvious policies or priorities which bear upon the land development process.

In the course of drafting the material which follows; indeed, in the course of drafting the major portion of this work as a whole, we have relied extensively on national legislation related to land use development. Such legislation is an important reference for anyone seeking to understand government goals concerning land use. Moreover, the parameters which control the present study have dictated that such legislation serve as our principal reference source. We believe it is worth stressing, however, that the lawyer or planner faced with the real life problem of drafting or implementing _particular_ rural land-use legislation for a _particular_ government having its own _particular_ personalities and political concerns, must look beyond the legislation in attempting to ascertain the policies or priorities upon which his or her efforts should be focused.

1. Social Policies

Inevitably, attainment of some degree of control over land use decision-making is intended to achieve one or more social policies. The substance of this policy, or policies, may be obvious and perhaps can be determined from discussions with government officials or a careful investigation of documents from which the outlines of a policy may emerge. Occasionally, however, the government's social goals respecting the use of land may be found in already existing legislation.

The point to be made here is that general social policies may serve to orient the land use decision-making process and thus may provide guidance in creating or implementing land use legislation. If, for example, the Government's social policy is to promote market incentives and to create a landed class of small holders, land use legislation which encourages collectivized state farming is unlikely to be warmly embraced. Similarly if the Government's policy is to encourage land-use decision-making at the local level, legislation which create a centralized planning and implementation infrastructure will likely be rejected or simply ignored. In short, while knowledge of the Government's social policies will not necessarily make the legislative drafter aware of all the curves, potholes and soft shoulders which may impede the drafting effort, at the least, such knowledge will keep the drafting effort on the right road.

An examination of land-related legislation discloses considerable variety in the social policies whose achievement is sought by way of controls upon land use and development. Such policies include, for instance, changes in land ownership patterns to correct abuses which developed during a prior period of colonization [10/]. The Government's social policy may also

---

10/ Frequently, achievement of such a policy may be sought through land-related controls which seek to reduce the maximum size of land holdings and limit the right of ownership to resident citizens. In Indonesia, for example, the Government's basic land legislation (Act No. 5 Concerning Basic Regulations on Agrarian Principles) declared that all rights on land have a social function. Ibid., Sec. 6. The legislation then goes to the heart of the tenure issue by providing that excessive ownership and control of land would not be permitted (Sec. 7), that only Indonesians henceforth would be granted full rights in land and that the Government was expressly directed to prevent monopolies in the agrarian sector (Secs. 9 (1)(2) and 13).

involve correcting the land tenure abuses of a prior regime; for instance, preventing or breaking up a monopoly of arable productive land controlled by a few citizens 11/, or socializing agrarian production through collectivization 12/. The control of land use or ownership may also be the means by which a government seeks to improve rural labor conditions and social security and to abolish ownership/tenancy relationships which, either de facto or de jure, bind the grant of the use of land to the rendering of personal service 13/.

11/ The basic land legislation of Algeria (Ordinance No. 71-73 on the Agrarian Revolution), for example, declares that the purpose of the agrarian revolution is to end the exploitation of man by man. For this purpose, it provides that only those who actually cultivate and develop land shall have rights to it and that the size of agrarian holdings shall be limited so as not to exceed the working capacity of the owner (Section 1). See also Section 5 of the Reclamation Act of 1902 (32 U.S. Stat 389, 43 U.S.C. para. 431) wherein the United States Congress sought to limit the monopolization of rural farmland by restricting the amount of federal subsidized irrigation water that could be purchased by a single individual to an amount sufficient to irrigate not more than 160 acres of land.

12/ Such an effort appears to lie at the heart of a series of proclamations and orders issued by the Government of Ethiopia on the subject of land use. In Proclamation 31 of 1975 providing for the Public Ownership of Rural Land, for example, the Government states its desire to correct specific land-related abuses including the "grabbing of considerable land by an insignificant number of feudal lords with the masses forced to live as serfs." Proclamation, p. 1.

Equally clear in its statement of the Government's goals regarding land, the same Proclamation declares its intent to promote inter alia:

1) the alteration of existing agrarian relations so that the peasant masses may be liberated from injustice, poverty or oppression;
2) the effectuation of a basic change in agrarian relations to emphasize work by cooperation , with the development of one (person) becoming the development of all;
3) the necessity of providing work for all rural people;
4) the necessity of providing participation.

In a subsequent proclamation (No. 71 of 1975, Organizing Peasants proclamation) the Government added to the foregoing the need to make peasants more concious and organized so that the revolution would realize its goals.

13/ See, e.g., the Peruvian Land Reform Act of 1969, Title I, para. 182.

It must be understood of course that social policies other than land tenure reform or the development of support for a new regime may drive the rural land use planning effort. Indeed, as the concept of planning the use of land has become more widespread, the social policy reasons for planning the use of land have expanded. Thus, for example, detailed land use plans have been proposed as a means to resolve conflicts between competing land users - particularly farmers, and livestock producers - over scarce land resources. They have also been created to provide better direction of demand for agricultural land for investment purposes [14/]. Similarly, land-control legislation has been proposed and enacted to ensure the participation of the general public in development decisions; to promote an equitable and balanced distribution of government sponsored development benefits; and to encourage the planning and implementation of development programmes at the local level [15/].

2. Preservation of Prime Agriculture Land

As population expands, there is increased pressure to convert prime agrarian land to other uses [16/]. Moreover, if agrarian land near urban areas is taxed on the principle of theoretical highest and best use, it is likely to suffer a greater tax burden than more distant agrarian land since the highest and best-use of land at the urban/rural interface is residential or commercial not agricultural. The result is that the owner of such land has a greater incentive to sell to developers or develop himself.

14/ The Central Regional Government of the Sudan in 1984 proposed the development of land use plans for the fertile lands of the Damazin and Roseries districts for precisely these reasons. See proposal of Central Region to FAO for Assistance in Land Use Planning, 1984.

15/ See Nepal, Decentralization Act 2039, Preamble.

16/ Extensive analysis of this effect has been undertaken by the World Watch Institute which has concluded, *inter alia*, that thousands of hectares of prime farmland are permanently disappearing from production each year because of urban expansion.

Unfortunately, such land - by virtue of its proximity - also possesses disproportionate agrarian benefits. Apart from its often prime character, such land offers the benefit of lower costs of transportation to market and thus lower prices to the consumer. To the extent it remains profitable, it also serves as a barrier to urban sprawl and eliminates or reduces reliance on more expensive food imports.

It thus behooves the lawyer or planner concerned with rural land use legislation to consider the issue of preserving prime agricultural land. It is unlikely that the government will have an expressed policy on the issue. Our review of agrarian-related legislation from more than 20 developing countries, for example, has failed to disclose even one instance where such legislation has focussed upon prime agricultural land and its preservation. Thus, there may be an obligation to introduce the issue to the government - if the loss of prime farmland is a problem. For the purpose of dealing with the issue in legislation, it may be sufficient to simply provide that one of the Government's goals is to maintain prime agricultural lands in agricultural use 17/. If the problem is especially severe, it may even be appropriate to establish a regulatory mechanism which inventories the existing stock of prime

---

17/ For instance, the Coastal Plan prepared by the California Coastal Zone Conservation Commission in 1976 attempts to guide future development of the State's scarce coastal land resources in accordance with the provisions of the Coastal Zone Conservation Act (Public Resources Code, Section 22000 et. seg.). When dealing with the subject of preserving scarce agricultural lands, the Plan provides :

> "Because coastal agriculture contributes substantially to state and national food supply and is a vital part of the State's economy, the State's goal shall be to maintain agricultural lands in agricultural production. Prime coastal agricultural lands... shall be maintained in agricultural use". California Coastal Plan, page 55.

After its adoption by the Legislature in 1977, the plan became the official policy of the State.

agricultural land and seeks to control non-agricultural development on such lands through, inter alia, the issuance of development permits 18/.

3. Consolidation or Subdivision of Land

The passage of time and the workings of customary - or statutory - inheritance practices not infrequently produce fragmented agrarian landholdings. Often the result is pattern of miniscule parcels which are too small to permit even subsistence farming, let alone practices which take advantage of economies of scale. The result, in turn, may be very low levels of productivity or simply the abandonment of otherwise productive farmland.

An important goal of the government's effort to plan the use of rural lands may thus be to consolidate fragmented rural holdings in order to improve production and restore profitability. In the context of the drafting of legislation, this may mean several things. On the one hand, it may require the imposition of a simple prohibition upon the subdivision of farmland below a certain size in order to prevent further fragmentation 19/. On the other hand, it may mean acting affirmatively to reduce the fragmentation of land by

---

18/ More extensive development control of this sort was attempted in the United States in 1976 when Assembly Bill 15 was introduced before the Legislature of California - the largest agricultural State and one of the states most subject to development pressure. As introduced, the bill would have established a regulatory mechanism that inventoried prime farmlands and then issued permits to control development on such lands in a manner consistent with principles and guidelines intended to restrict the impact of development. The bill failed to pass the Legislature; it serves, however, as a model for legislation concerned with achieving the goal of prime agricultural land preservation.

19/ In Peru, for example, the Land Reform Act of 1969 prohibits the subdivision of rural landholdings into less than 3 hectares or, in the alternative, into an area less than that designated by the Government as being suitable for a "family agricultural unit". Land Reform Act, Title VIII, Section 98.

A less precise restriction is found in Belize where Ordinance No. 16 (1981) places procedural controls on the subdivision of land. While the law does not contain substantive standards to guide the determination of when land subdivision will be approved, the procedural controls nonetheless suggest that the subdivision of land will be scrutinized and is not unrestricted.

increasing the size of holdings and eliminating small parcels and dual ownerships so that, for each owner, there is formed one holding of sufficient size and proper shape as to allow economically viable exploitation for agricultural purposes [20/]. Where sufficient government landholdings are available, such an enlargement process may actually involve the resettlement of small holders in land settlement projects [21/]. Where government landholdings are not extensive, the process of enlargement may necessarily be more gradual, with compensation perhaps being paid to those small holders whose lands are absorbed into larger more suitable holdings [22/].

20/ See, for example, the Cyprus Land Consolidation Law (1969), Section 2. To effectuate such a policy the Cyprus legislation creates a Land Consolidation Authority and provides that the Authority may pursue the consolidation of land by one of three methods : 1) the owner's mutual agreement, 2) a statutory resolution by the owners involved and 3) by government order under the statute.

21/ In Peru, for example, the Land Reform Act authorizes the government to determine the boundaries of areas plagued with minifurdios (very small holdings) in order that the population within such areas may be endowed with land under rural land settlement projects carried out by the State, with preference being given to areas adjacent to the region where consolidation is going forward. Land Reform Act, Title VIII, Secs. 102 and 107. Similarly, Uruguay, Act No. 13.667 concerning soil conservation, provides that in carrying out land consolidation projects in areas of erosion and unsound soil use, the Ministry of Agriculture shall promote conservation projects in "newly consolidated farming units".

22/ The basic land legislation of Indonesia - a country afflicted with small holdings, particularly on the island of Java - provides, for example, that the minimum area of land which may be utilized by a family shall be regulated and that the minimum limit shall be obtained through a "gradual process". Act No. 5 (24 September 1960), Sec. 17. The Act does not detail precisely how such a gradual process should operate, however. Most certainly it does not describe the extensive transmigrational undertaking which Indonesia has subsequently employed to resettle Javanese small holders to government land settlement projects in Sumatra.

4. Control of Agricultural Development Impacts Upon Other Uses

Land use planning legislation may also serve to implement - or create - government policies which are designed to limit the detrimental impact of certain agricultural activities.

For instance, legislation may recognize the destructive impacts of shifting cultivation and serve to implement a policy of opposition to such practices by establishing prohibitions against the burning of brush or undergrowth, timber and standing plant cover [23/]. It may even make anyone engaging in such practices subject to criminal penalties [24/]. Also, legislation may attempt to limit the impact of agricultural activities on water resources; for example, by controlling agricultural development in valuable watershed areas [25/] or limiting the damage from agriculturally-related non-point sources of water pollution such as the run-off of toxic chemicals or silt [26/].

Also, for the purpose of drafting or implementing legislation, it is useful to consider whether there is, or should be a government policy to limit the impact of activities by some agriculturalists upon the activities of other

---

23/ See, e.g., the Rwanda Soil and Conservation Act, 1982, Section 5.

24/ *Ibid.*, Section 12.

25/ A proposed Water Resources Act for Western Samoa, for example, authorizes the creation of watershed protection "zones" and, through the establishment of such "zones", gives government the legal power to control development, including placing restrictions on the "type or method of farming which may be undertaken" on lands within such zones. Draft, Water Resources Act (1985), Section 54. See also proposed Water Resources Act for Tonga (1985), Section 59; draft Waters Enactment of Malaysia (1984), Section 26.

26/ 1972 amendments to the Federal Water Pollution Control Act in the United States, for example, establish "area-wide waste management plans" which, *inter alia*, are required to 1) identify agriculturally related non-point sources of pollution including return flows from irrigated agriculture and their cumulative effects, runoff from manure disposal areas and from land used for livestock and crop production and 2) set forth procedures and methods (including land-use requirements) to control such sources to the extent feasible. FWPCA para. 208 (2)(F).

agriculturalists. Thus, if the encroachment of mechanized farms upon lands used by pastoralists for forage is a problem, consideration ought to be given to dealing with the problem through proposed land use legislaton. Similarly, if farmers, or others, are encroaching upon forest lands seeking either fuel or undepleted soils, it may be appropriate to orient proposed land-use legislation toward government support of a programme of reforestation 27/, creation of forest reserve areas and the monitoring and enforcing prohibitions against encroachments.

5. Food Production or Export Crops

A policy choice which confronts the governments of many developing countries is whether to encourage agricultural activities that contribute to the supply of food necessary to meet domestic demand or, instead, to encourage the production of commodities for export. Ideally, of course, agriculture should do both : it should serve domestic needs and produce the foreign exchange necessary to purchase needed goods from others. Frequently, however, the agricultural sector of a developing country lacks the capacity to produce significant export revenue while simultaneously serving domestic consumers. Hence the government is compelled to make a policy choice.

The nature of that choice may have a considerable impact upon any legislation which is intended to regulate the use of land. A decision to emphasize export commodities, for instance, may necessitate wholesale changes in the scale upon which agricultural activities are conducted. It may prove more efficient - and thus more competitive - to produce a crop such as cotton, for example, in a manner which takes advantage of the economies of scale that can be provided by large agricultural plots and more extensive use of mechanized equipment. Relevant land use legislation thus may be directed at

---

27/ The Rwanda Soil Conservation Act of 1982, for example, provides that degraded land which is unsuitable for crop or animal husbandry purposes shall be afforested. Further, it provides that the felling of national forests and other wooded stands shall proceed only in conformity with the regulations in force. Soil Conservation Act, Sec. 4.

eliminating small holdings and consolidating land ownerships or reserving land more suitable for machinery to the production of certain crops. It may also be directed at allocating land near infrastructural facilities, such as ports or railways or paved roads, for agricultural export activities.

A decision to pursue an export-led agricultural economy may also involve major changes in the inputs which are provided to farmers. The production of certain crops, for example, may be feasible only if a source of water is available year round. Thus, the provision of irrigation water - and attendant dams, reservoirs and canals - becomes significant. Upon whose lands are such facilities to be located, and whose rights to water are to be impaired so that export farmers may have such a supply ? Moreover, farmland inevitably varies in terms of productivity : some land is highly productive prime land; most is not. Should prime farmland be reserved for the production of crops which produce significant export revenue, should it be set aside for the production of staple crops necessary to feed the country's own citizens or should the owners of such land be permitted to choose which crops will be grown ? The response may well determine whether the government's chosen policy is frustrated or fulfilled.

6. Compulsory Tilling of Agricultural Land and Controls on Soil Depletion

Not infrequently, developing countries face problems concerning the intensity of use of land. On the one hand, land may be overgrazed, it may be planted with crops which impoverish the soil, or it may be unprotected from the effects of wind or rain. On the other hand, arable land may be underutilized because it is held by absentee owners, because it is beyond the capacity of a resident working owner, or because it has an uneconomical size, shape or location. In these circumstances, there may exist government policies concerning controls on soil depletion or the compulsory tilling of land.

a) Soil Depletion and Erosion

Occasionally the problems of soil depletion and erosion are expressly made the subject of government policy [28/]. Often, however, although these problems touch virtually all sectors of the community, they are not recognized as specific problems in themselves - something which constitutes a major obstacle to achieving land conservation.

In essence, soil erosion and depletion are most effectively controlled by prevention, which in turn depends upon using land within its capability for sustained production [29/]. These two elements have been recognized as the cornerstones of a land conservation policy which, in order to be effective, should involve frequent review of such things as : 1) the value of production in areas afflicted with depletion or erosion, 2) the urgency of remedial action measured in terms of the rate at which degradation

---

28/ For example, Act No. 13.667 of Uruguay (1968) declares soil conservation to be a subject that is in the national interest. Section 2 of the legislation, in fact, provides that agricultural producers shall apply on their farms such methods as the Ministry of Agriculture may prescribe in order to prevent the loss or deterioration of soils or to bring about their reclamation. Section 3 of that same law then gives the Ministry of Agriculture various detailed responsibilities to coordinate and direct soil conservation activities, while Section 7 gives the Ministry the responsibility to establish soil conservation projects in different "regions" - a term which is defined in the law as a geographical area whose boundaries are designated in such a way that an "integrated approach" is taken to soil conservation in areas where soils are used in such a manner that damage is likely to result or has already occured from erosion or improper soil use.

That same Section of the Uruguyan law also evidences considerable sophistication in training and correcting the root causes of soil degradation by requiring the Ministry of Agriculture to carry out surveys and studies to ascertain the physical, social and economic causes of damage to soils and to determine the most suitable methods of conservation conducive to soil conservation planning. Law No. 13.667 (Section 7).

29/ See J. Dixon "Comments on the Preparation of a Master Plan for Soil Conservation In Turkey", p. 5, FAO, November, 1984.

is proceeding, 3) the difficulty and cost of treatment at some future time if degradation is allowed to continue and 4) acceptable standards of land management under differing economic cicumstances 30/. In order to keep these and other factors under fairly frequent review, it has been suggested also that there should exist a legally constituted administrative body possessing a broad mandate to :

- appraise the condition of soil resources on a continuing basis;

- develop and pursue the implementation of programmes for the protection of soil resources; and

- coordinate the programmes of all government departments using or preserving land resources 31/.

Exactly <u>how</u> government programmes should be coordinated to protect soil resources and precisely what standards and programmes will be used in the appraisal and protection of soil resources will vary from case to case. It may be sufficient, for example, for land development legislation to condition land ownership upon a general obligation to protect the land from erosion 32/. On the other hand, it may be important to take a more comprehensive approach and provide for detailed erosion-related obligations to be met by land

---

30/ See J. Dixon "Comments on the Preparation of a Master Plan for Soil Conservation In Turkey", p. 5, FAO, November, 1984.

31/ <u>Ibid.</u>

32/ Indonesia's Act No. 5 concerning basic regulations on agrarian principles (1960) provides in section 15, for example, that the prevention of damage to land is the duty of every person, corporation or organization having legal relations with the land. In Section 27 the Act goes on to provide that the right of ownership in land is "annulled" if the land is "destroyed". Thus, there is a very tangible incentive not to allow soil erosion to take place. Similarly, Sections 34 and 40 provide, respectively, for amendment of the right to exploit and to build if the land is destroyed.

owners [33/]. A middle course would be to set forth the obligation to prevent erosion and to provide for primary implementation of the statutory language by the state in accordance with regulations adopted for this purpose

---

33/ In Rwanda, for example, a very comprehensive law has been adopted on the subjects of soil conservation, protection and use. Act No. 11/82 (1982). Section 1 of the Act makes it mandatory for every farmer to,

> "provide and maintain arrangements for the control of wind erosion and avoid any degradation of the soil through human agency."

The same section also directs that farmers should "avoid overstocking and degrading pastureland".

In Section 2, the Act provides that there be erosion control arrangements such as reseeding, tree planting and arrangements for the evacuation of water. in the case of a mine or quarry, Section 3 of the Act provides that the concession holder shall be required to provide and maintain erosion control arrangements, replace tree cover on land degraded by erosion and take steps to assure that farmland or other land is not impaired by the accumulation of waste or the evacuation of wastewater. Section 4, in turn, provides that the felling of trees may proceed only in conformity with regulations in force.

Finally, section 6 of the Act establishes a Soil Conservation and Use Commission within each prefecture of the country for the purpose of 1) giving technical advice to anyone who comes within the terms of the Act and 2) advising the Minister having responsibility for soil conservation on any matter having to do with safeguarding soil resources. External measures are also provided for the enforcement of the terms of the Act against persons who fail to carry out their responsibilities under the Act.

by the agency charged with enforcement of the basic law 34/.

On the other hand, the Government may have - or may need - a more focussed soil protection policy which should be given expression by the lawyer or planner. For example, where mining activities are extensive, it may be

---

34/ The Belize Land Utilisation Ordinance of 1981, for example, provides that the Minister of Government responsible for land may - for the better utilization of land - make regulations to provide for such measures as may be required to prevent erosion.

Act No. 13.667 of Uruguay dealing with soil erosion, on the other hand, takes a somewhat different approach. After declaring soil conservation to be in the national interest, the Act makes it the responsibility of the State to provide for the prevention and control of erosion and the loss of soils (Section 1) and merely the "duty" of others to "collaborate" with the State in these matters (Section 2). However, agricultural producers "shall" apply on their farms such methods as are prescribed by the Ministry of Agriculture in order to prevent the loss or deterioration of soils or to bring about their reclamation.

Under the terms of the Uruguayan Soils Act, the Ministry of agriculture is given responsibility for a wide variety of things, including : 1) coordinating and directing all activities designed to ensure sound soil management, 2) the establishment of soil conservation and reclamation projects in such a way that an integrated approach is taken to soil conservation in areas where soils have been or could be damaged, 3) carrying out surveys in soil conservation regions in order to ascertain the physical, social or economic causes of soil damage and 4) initiating regional soil conservation programmes designed to rectify soil damage. In addition, the Act provides for the development of a "soil and Water Conservation Plan" which describes: 1) the area or property affected, 2) proposed soil conservation works, 3) soil conservation practices to be followed by participating farmers and 4) establishment of a regional committee to act as an advisory body to the Ministry of Agriculture. Basically, the regional soil conservation committee publicizes and promotes soil and water conservation in the region; it also has the power, however, to evaluate soil conservation projects within the region and to decide on measures conducive to the efficient implementation of those projects (Section 10). Each regional soil conservation project, however, remains the legal responsibility of the local office of the Ministry of Agriculture (Section 11).

Finally, in addition to the statutory powers already detailed above, the Uruguayan law also provides that where land has been seriously damaged by continuously worsening erosion and cannot be restored by private individuals because of the magnitude of the work involved, the Government may expropriate the land (Section 12). For this purpose, "continuously worsening erosion" means the "regular loss every year of a notable portion of the soil mantle as a result of water or wind action" (Section 13).

important to provide for the restoration of mined areas 35/. Or, it may be important to create buffer zones which will protect sensitive soils from grazing activities. By creating a null zone around sensitive lands, the legislation will discourage encroachment by wandering cattle or errant farmers 36/.

Similarly, government may be confronting a problem of salt build-up in otherwise valuable soils; thus, there may (or should) be a policy of protecting land through limits on the salinity of water applied to crops on such lands or through the requirement of drainage measures sufficient to ensure that salts will be flushed and carried to less valuable areas 37/.

35/ See, e.g., Section 3 of Rwanda's Act number 11/82 (1982) relative to soil protection, conservation and land use, wherein it is provided that restoration of the land shall be provided for by the owner of a mine or quarry.

36/ Legislation enacted in Cameroon (Forestry, Wildlife and Fishery Law of 1981) for example, gives the Government the power to create buffer zones around protected forest areas. While nothing specific is said about the prevention of erosion, the concept of using buffer zones to protect sensitive soils would appear to be just as viable.

37/ No legislation has been found which deals precisely with this topic in great detail. Nevertheless, it is possible to argue that Regulations for the Preservation of Water Resources, adopted by Saudi Arabian Royal Decree No. 34 (1980) give the Ministry of Agriculture and Water the authority to prevent salt build-up on valuable lands by repairing or closing wells which, _inter alia_, "_lead to soil damage_" (Section 5).

The problem of salt buildup is a major concern in the Great Central Valley of the Western United States, where the periodic application of relatively high chloride content water over several decades has resulted in the abandonment of thousands of hectares of once productive lands. It has also prompted farmers to lay hundreds of kilometers of drain tiles (without legislative compulsion) and provided impetus to congressional authorization of a proposed drain channel that will take heavily salt-polluted agricultural wastewater out of the valley. Where the drain canal will _discharge_ that water, however, is a question plaguing planners in the state and, illustrates the kind of resource use issues that can arise in connection with efforts to lower the salinity content of soils. Current plans envision the discharge of agricultural wastewater to San Francisco Bay. Environmentalists, however, are likely to oppose that plan as well as other proposals to discharge wastewater into the Pacific Ocean. Until these matters can be resolved, the canal and thus the build-up of salts in valuable farmlands, are likely to remain unresolved issues.

In a like manner, the lawyer or planner should evaluate whether there exists or is a need for controls necessary to restrict grazing activities and provide for the restoration of overgrazed areas 38/. Finally, if desertification due to overgrazing or other causes, is a problem confronting the government, it is appropriate to investigate whether the government has developed a policy to deal with the problem and, if not, whether land use legislation presents on appropriate means for establishing such a policy and implementing it 39/.

The point to be made here is that soil depletion or erosion is likely to be a subject upon which the government should have a reasonably detailed policy position, even if no such position has been formally expressed. It is a subject, in short, upon which the lawyer or planner should focus attention when considering how to orient the government's request for an effective programme of land use planning.

38/ Botswana, for example, has adopted the Agricultural Resources Conservation Act of 1974 which authorizes the Agricultural Resources Board created by the law to issue "Conservation Orders". Such orders may be directed to the owner or occupier of any land and may require the person to undertake such measures as the Agricultural Resources Board deems necessary to conserve the agricultural resources on such land. Those resources are defined to include soils (Section 16). To protect soils, such Conservation Orders may, among other things,

> "prohibit, regulate, require or control
>
> ...
>
> (ii) the grazing or watering of livestock". (Id. Section 16).

See also Section 1 of Act No. 11/82 of Rwanda which makes it "mandatory" for every farmer to "avoid overstocking and degrading pasture land".

39/ The Agricultural Resources Conservation Act of Botswana (1974), cited above, also appears directed at the problem of desertification. *Inter alia*, it requires afforestation, reforestation, the fencing of land and the protection of slopes and catchment areas, "for the protection of vegetation".

b) Underutilized land

The chronic underutilization of land may result from a variety of causes that range from social and economic conditions on the one hand to physical circumstances on the other. It may be that underutilization is the result of a high degree of absentee ownership - itself the result of a variety of social, economic or political factors. Thus, the problems of under utilization may be the focus of a government policy which should be pursued through appropriate land-use legislation.

Such legislation, for example, may seek to encourage agrarian development projects which pursue a programme of "Land to the Tiller". Or the legislation may provide the authority for government to expropriate absentee-owned land - or land which exceeds the farming ability of resident owners [40/] - for re-distribution to new resident owners who have the capability to farm more aggressively [41/]. Or, finally, to guide the land development process, such legislation may set forth the principle that every

---

40/ Algerian Ordinance No. 71-73 on Agrarian Revolution Principles is an example of such legislation. It provides that the land belongs to those who work it (Section 1) and that the rights of land owners to the land will be abolished where those owners do not actually participate in production. It also provides for the loss of rights where owners neglect to use the land (Section 2). Moreover the legislation states that the size of agrarian holdings shall be limited in such a way that they do not exceed the working capacity of the owner and his family (*Ibid*., Section 2).

41/ Peruvian Act No. 17.716, the Land Reform Act (1969), sets forth a list of examples in which land is not being used in accordance with the social interest and includes the abandonment of land or its inefficient working. If it is so listed, all such land may, under the terms of the Act, be taken over by the government following expropriation proceedings. It may then be reallocated to settlers by the Department of Land Reform and Land Settlement (Article 15).

person holding an interest in agrarian land is obliged to farm that land himself 42/.

Where, on the other hand, the underutilization of land results from legal or physical impediments, the task may be to design legislation which removes the barrier directly - if it is legal in character - or provides the government with the legal authority necessary to tackle the barrier - if it is physical. For example, if the law has previously allowed the generous leasing of government land, the result may be the creation of a small class of persons controlling disproportionately large blocks of underutilized land and the denial of access to persons genuinely desiring to farm. The solution may be to change the law to provide for a ceiling on the amount of land held - or controlled - by an individual 43/. Or, where land is underutilized because official government purchase policies fail to provide farmers with sufficient monetary incentives to farm - either because commodity prices fail to reflect current farming costs or because the government simply wants to maximize

---

42/ Act No. 5 of Indonesia ("concerning basic regulations on agrarian principles") contains such a statement - and even extends it to "corporate bodies" (Section 10). Perhaps recognizing the difficulty of literally applying such a principle to corporate persons, however, the legislation notes that the requirement of working owners exists "in principle" and then provides that it shall be implemented through more detailed regulations. The literal application of such a principle to corporate farmers would, no doubt, be difficult, if not impossible. On the other hand, the existence of such a principle in relevant land-use legislation might also provide the legal authority necessary to transfer ownership from corporations to otherwise landless farm workers.

43/ Such a problem, for example, developed over a long period in Guyana where the generous leasing of public land encouraged the accumulation of land by a few. See Rath and Okoth-Ogendo, Agrarian Reform Planning and Legislation for Guyana, FAO, TCP/GUY/2201, p. 17. The proposed solution has been to impose a statutory ceiling on the lands held under lease by a particular individual. Moreover, existing legislation was recommended to be changed to establish a programme of enfranchisement of tenants - with the intention of creating a new, and much more extensive, landed class having an ownership interest in land and thus the incentive to farm that land more intensively. See Rath and Okoth-Ogendo, Ibid., p. 19.

revenues from export crops [44/] - the legislation may have to focus upon statutory changes in policy which will generate a larger farm income and thus more intensive use of farmland. On the other hand, where land is underutilized because necessary inputs such as water are lacking - a physical impediment inotherwords - it is important that the government be provided with the legal authority to arrange for such inputs where it is feasible to do so.

7. Preservation and Enhancement of Forest Reserves

Previously we have discussed orienting land use legislation in a manner which serves to promote a policy of protecting forest resources from the impacts of other agricultural activities. Government policy to protect and enhance forest resources may also be effected through more direct measures and it thus behooves the lawyer or planner to consider how best to meet the government's needs.

When a country has significant forest resources, it is also likely to have legislation - sometimes dating from colonial days - which in theory is intended to protect the resource and ensure its availability for future generations. In fact, however, such dated legislation is likely to be ineffective. Rather than treating forests as a sustainable but harvestible resource which may be used for multiple purposes, the legislation is more likely to provide for the creation of forest enclaves to be defended against attack from various quarters. Unfortunately, the defenders - who are typically employees of a central or regional forestry department - are usually far outnumbered by those desiring to use the forests. The result is that the forest enclaves are not well defended and are gradually being eroded by those wishing to expand their farmland or graze their animals or gather their fuel. An alternative scenario sometimes sees the government itself encouraging the rapid exploitation of forest reserves by citizens or outsiders as a means of earning foreign exchange. That the exploitation may take place in a forest reserve is a secondary consideration.

44/ See Rath and Okoth-Ogendo, Agrarian Reform Planning and Legislation for Guyana, TCP/GUY/2201, p. 8.

Thus, rather than being written on a clean slate, land use legislation directed at forest policy is more likely to consist of a new approach to the implementation of a policy that has already been addressed in the law. In essence, the new approach consists of an effort to make the country's land-use legislation more "appropriate" in dealing with the threats posed to the nations' forests. Rather than simply establishing forest reserves and erecting unenforceable prohibitions, for example, land use legislation may instead encourage a programme which provides government benefits or protections to landowners who maintain timber stands [45/]. Similarly the legislation may encourage re-forestation by private persons [46/] or public entities [47/] in order to provide for a sustained yield; indeed, the legislation may make the re-planting of trees a condition of any contract or government authorization to harvest timber [48/].

45/ See, for example, Cameroon Law No. 81-13 (1981) which provides that private forests (and accompanying government protections) may result from plantations.

46/ In Tanzania, for example, the Forestry Ordinance of 1982 empowers the Director of Forestry to make covenants with landowners, which covenants have as their objective the setting aside of certain portions of land for commercial tree growing in accordance with sound forestry practices. Subject to certain conditions, the covenants are made enforceable against the coventor and his successors in interest.

Similarly, Tanzania administrative circular No. 1986 (1980) provides for two alternative approaches which may be carried out under the supervision of the Department of Environment, Nature Protection and Tourism : 1) the person or company engaged in timber harvesting carries out reforestation on its own within the zone for which the timber harvesting contract is granted or 2) the person or company maintains a forest nursery and provides infrastructural support to the reforestation units of the forest administration which operates in the same region. In addition each person or company who harvests timber must prepare a 3 year or 5 year reforestation programme in collaboration with the regional departments to which the reforestation units belong. The granting or renewal of timber harvesting permits is possible only if the reforestation programme is implemented.

47/ Congo Law No. 004/74 (as amended in 1982), for example, directs that reforestation is to be carried out by a specialized state agency while the expenses of reforestation and forest management are financed by a forestry development fund.

48/ See, e.g., Zaire Administrative Circular No. 1986 (1980).

Utilizing a somewhat different approach, land use legislation may also seek to encourage agro-forestry or other multiple-use activities that are compatible with, or even dependent upon, forest resources 49/. As an example, a legal requirement that requires the local processing of forest produce not only will provide for rural employment; it will also encourage the creation of industries whose long-term viability depends upon a sustained yield of locally produced forest products.

Finally, in areas where unauthorized access to forest lands is more tightly controlled, it may be possible to encourage conservation of forest resources by means of legislation which manipulates timber harvesting through the application of one or more tax policies. For instance, legislation may provide for the establishment of a reforestation fund and assure its financing by means of a revenue tax on cut timber, a transport tax on the transport of sawn logs to market or an export tax on logs or processed forest products - or any combination of such taxes 50/. By varying the rate so as to tax processed wood at a level which is substantially lower than that imposed on the export of unprocessed materials, the tax legislation may encourage local processing - and thus local industry which is again dependent upon a long-term sustained yield of forest products 51/.

49/ For example. guidelines adopted by the United States Forest Service (47 Fed. Register 190, p. 43026 et. seg.) require the preparation of a forest plan which sets forth "multiple use goals" and "multiple use prescriptions and associated standards and guidelines" for a forest management area. Guidelines, Section 219.11. "Multiple use" is in turn defined by the guidelines as,

> "The management of all the various renewable surface resources of the National Forest System so that they are utilized in the combination that will best meet the need of the American people; making the most judicious use of the land for some or all of these resources or related services over areas large enough to private sufficient latitude for periodic adjustments in use to conform to changing needs and conditions."

50/ Zaire, Ordinance No. 244 (1979) provides for just such a timber tax system.

51/ Ordinance No. 82.71 and Law No. 81-127 adopted by the Ivory Coast provide recent (1981) examples of government imposed tax incentives to process forest produce locally. The Law, for instance, determines the export tax rates on processed woods (sawn wood, veneer and plywood) and provides for rates which are considerably lower than those applicable to unprocessed woods.

In sum, it is likely that a country with substantial forest resources will have a policy favoring a long-term sustained yield. However, it is possible that existing legislation which is intended to implement such policy is not "appropriate" to the task and thus fails to achieve the result which is sought. Accordingly, it is imperative that the lawyer or planner not simply accept such legislation at face value, but instead look behind the surface to see if the legislation works. If it does not produce the result for which it was intended, the opportunity to draft land use legislation should then be viewed as presenting the additional opportunity of producing more "appropriate" controls which will better achieve the governments' goals for its forest resources. The examples cited in this section serve to indicate the variety of approaches that can be utilized in pursuing that end.

8. Policies Concerning Indigenous Populations

In the previous sections of this chapter we have mainly discussed the importance of ascertaining and implementing government policies concerning inanimate natural resources such as agricultural lands, forests and fragile and threatened soils, among others. The importance of these resources, while undeniable, should nonetheless not be allowed to obscure the importance of development, and its sometimes adverse impacts, to people and the environment they share with other animate creatures. This is especially so with regard to the rural poor whose customary rights and practices are often at odds with government sponsored efforts to develop rural lands.

Several commentators [52/] have outlined a series of standard criteria which are recommended for use in making an appraisal of the impacts

---

52/ Conyers and Hills, An Introduction to Development Planning in the Third World, Wiley and Sons (1984), p. 143, citing G. Cochrane, The Cultural Appraisal of Development Projects (Praeger, 1979). Conyers and Hills provide an excellent theoretical as well as how to discussion regarding land-use planning and are recommended for reading by anyone faced with the prospect of designing or implementing a land-use planning system.

of development upon specific cultural groups. The criteria are suggested as part of a larger and more general effort to make a social impact analysis (SIA) of the adverse effects of development activities. Broadly applicable to a variety of cultural and social groups, they are especially useful in discovering, implementing (or creating) government policies regarding indigenous people. In brief, these criteria should relate to the following :

1. Identification of social groups. The legislation should require relevant land use planning officials to first undertake a determination of which groups - particularly tribal groups of indigenous peoples - there are and where they are located;

2. Patterns of social organization. In addition, there should be an analysis of the structure of each identified indigenous group for the purpose of ascertaining who holds political power, how decisions are made and how disputes are resolved;

3. Belief systems. A proper analysis of development impacts upon indigenous groups should also investigate the belief system of each group, particularly as such system relates to the use of land and water resources;

4. Wealth systems. It also is important to understand cultural practices regarding wealth forms and how wealth is accumulated. If, for example, cattle constitue a form of wealth and the accumulation of cattle is viewed as a desirable goal, this customary practice may have a significant impact upon (or, in turn, be significantly impacted by) a land development programme oriented to the protection or rehabilitation of overgrazed rangelands;

5. Patterns of mobility. The migratory patterns of indigenous people can also have a highly significant impact upon land development decisions or, conversely, be impacted by such decisions. A land development programme, for example, that

proposes the development of migratory rangelands for rainfed agriculture could, unless appropriate precautions are taken, result in the interruption of migratory patterns with highly adverse consequences for nomadic peoples. Conversely, the frustration of rainfed agriculture goals could be caused by nomads who continue to pasture their cattle without regard to the government's efforts to demarcate land for rainfed purposes. In either event, avoidable clashes between competing interests are likely to result.

6. Access to basic human needs. Finally if indigenous peoples are not to be by-passed - or worse, trampled - by land development, it is essential that the access of such people to the means of satisfying basic human needs be evaluated before land development plans are established in final form. What do such needs include ? At a minimum, they would appear to involve the availability of clean water; a source of healthful food in suitable quantities, adequate shelter and, protection from physical danger. An expanded list would include basic medical care and educational facilities, among other things. To the extent these basic human needs of indigenous people are considered, it is more likely that land use decisions can be structured to preserve or provide the means of satisfying such needs. Conversely, if basic human needs are ignored, it is entirely possible that land development will not only fail to benefit indigenous peoples but, instead, may become the instrument which deprives such people of the means of their existence.

In sum, providing in legislation that the above criteria be used to perform a cultural appraisal as part of the land use planning process before land development is undertaken, is an important way in which the cultural values and basic needs of indigenous peoples can be protected. Even if all of the values of such peoples are not preserved in their entirety, a land use decision-making process which includes such values among the elements to be considered, is less likely to foment conflicts between important social groups than a decision-making process which proceeds in ignorance of such values.

9. Policies Concerning Protection of the Environment from Land Development Impacts

Finally, it is likely that the Government may (or should) have a policy concerning protection of the environment from the adverse impacts of land development. While the legal approach to environmental protection is almost certain to vary according to the specific circumstances of each country, or region in issue, some light can nonetheless be shed by a broad consideration of the subject.

In general, three differing legal approaches lend themselves to implementation of a government's intention to protect the environment from land development impacts. They are : 1) the creation of reserves, including parks, in order to directly provide a protected sanctuary for wildlife, scenic attractions or other environmental amenities; 2) creation of an environmental impact analysis procedure which requires the assessment and comparison of specific proposed development projects and alternatives; and 3) the development of a regulatory system which, by permit, license or other mechanism, attempts to limit the adverse impacts of existing or proposed land development.

a) The Creation of Protected Areas

The most direct approach to the preservation of wildlife or scenic resources is the establishment of protected areas where some or all development activities are controlled. In the past, the tendency was to simply set aside certain land as a reserve and thus bar all development activity. Such an approach generally failed, however, for several reasons. First, where the reserved land was privately owned or tribal in character, creating a reserve was extremely expensive. Not only would other laws frequently provide for the payment of compensation, but also the government might be obliged - for statutory or political reasons - to undertake a programme of land exchange or resettlement. In addition, even if a reserve was created, enforcing the restrictions applicable in the reserve could be difficult. One person's national park is another person's reserve of fuelwood and edible game, and unless well policed, reserves would suffer raiding and poaching, particularly when times were hard in nearby areas. Nor was the raiding and poaching necessarily just a local matter. If the national government faced a revenue crisis that could be diminished or averted by quick increases in the export of raw materials, attention often fell on the national resources legislatively locked-up in reserves. In sum, reserves were often anything but 53/.

As a result of the problems which followed the creation of national reserves, increased sophistication is now used in some jurisdictions when the reserve approach is chosen for natural resource protection. For instance, rather than simply providing for the creation of a "reserve", some countries make provision for the creation of different kinds of protected areas. A single law, for example, may authorize the creation of wildlife management zones, protected wildlife areas, national parks and fully protected nature and wildlife reserves 54/. For each category of reserve, the law may impose different limitations upon development activities within or near the reserve. Thus, for example, the law may establish a reserve but nevertheless allow agro-forestry activities, limited collection of firewood or even some hunting.

The advantage of such a graduated approach is several-fold. First, it avoids the problems which may result when a reserve with a "Do not touch" sign firmly attached is dangled in front of the local population. By authorizing compatible uses which depend for their success upon restricted access and the exclusion of certain development activities, the more sophisticated approach to reserves attempts to create local interest groups whose economic

---

53/ While we have used the past tense to describe the problems facing wildlife and scenic reserves, the described situation still exists in a variety of venues and can be detected without much difficulty.

54/ Law No. 1/82 of Gabon (the Forest Law) for example, makes provision for the establishment of each of the protected areas described in the text. The law also regulates the administration and utilization of wildlife management zones, the exercise of hunting rights and the possession, transport and export of game and trophies.

well-being depends upon the success of the protected area. Enforcement of the restrictions of the protected area is thus more likely to occur since it is now a matter of local concern, not just a policing problem of interest to national officials residing many kilometers away.

In addition, an approach to environmental protection which authorizes limited development where such development is "appropriate", may well make the creation of protected areas more feasible economically. The law of eminent domain is far from static. Indeed, legislative efforts to improve environmental quality over the past 15 to 20 years through the creation of green belts and open space plans, down-zoning and zoning moratoriums among others, have caused an explosion in the development of legal principles concerning the right to compensation. In those jurisdictions which have faced frequent litigation on the subject, it appears that among the principles which are emerging is the view that no "taking" - and thus no right to compensation - occurs unless and until government intrusion on the rights of the property owner results in a total loss of the value of the affected parcel [55/]. The practical effect is that government may permissibly regulate the use of land in a protected area without buying it, so long as it permits some compatible use of the land by its owners. It is only when government destroys the economic value of the land to its owner by prohibiting all activity (an open-space easement for example) that government may be obliged to pay compensation. Thus, by authorizing some commercial useful activities, the more sophisticated approach to environmental reserves may produce the additional benefit of economic feasibility from the government's point of view.

Finally, efforts to intertwine wildlife and scenic protection with compatible economic uses may tend to discourage government sponsored raiding when the need arises for increased export revenues. Because some economic uses may be occuring, it will not be so easy to single out protected areas as non contributing sectors of the economy which may be exploited. Moreover, if some compatible uses are occuring, officials may be more hesitant to exploit

---

55/ See, e.g., Sierra Terreno v. Tahoe Regional Planning Agency, 79 Cal. App. 3d 439; HFH Ltd. v. Superior Court 15 Cal. 3d 508; Agins v. City of Tiburon 24 Cal. 3d 266.

reserves and thus incur the animosity of the persons whose livelihood depends upon the reserve's integrity. Particularly is this so when those uses are taking place in accordance with a government sponsored and approved plan 56/.

56/ The notion of planning the use of protected areas is also finding its way into more enlightened legislation. Law No. 81-13 (1981) of Cameroon, for example, lays down forestry, wildlife and fisheries regulations for the country in a well structured fashion. Part I of the law lays out objectives which include conservation, development and exploitation of wildlife. Part II of the law then classifies lands (mainly forest lands) into functional categories such as integral nature reserves and parks, wild animal and plant sanctuaries and state game ranches. It then requires the preparation of a management plan for each state forest and natural park in accordance with the designation of the area.

Presidential Decree No. 1152 of the Philippines (Philippine Environment Code, 1974) also requires planning directed at sensitive areas; however, the planning is to occur at the macro-level rather than locally. Specifically Title III of the law dealing with "Land use Management" requires preparation of a "Land Use Scheme" by the Human Settlements Commission for consideration by the government's National Environmental Protection Council. *Inter alia,* the plan is to include,

> "a method of identification of areas where uncontrolled development could result in irreparable damage to important historic, cultural or aesthetic values or natural systems or processes of national significance." (See 23 (d)).

Further, the law provides that in the location of industrial establishments, the regulating and enforcing agencies of the government shall take into account "the social, economic, geographic and significant environmental impact of said establishments." (Section 24). Finally, in Title IV dealing with "Natural Resources Management and Conservation" the law requires the Department of Natural Resources to,

> "establish a system of rational exploitation and conservation of wildlife resources and encourage citizen participation in the maintenance and/or enhancement of their continuous productivity". (*Ibid.*, Section 28).

Such measures are then statutorily defined to include :

a) regulation of the marketing of threatened wildlife resources,

b) reviewing existing rules on the exploitation of wildlife so as to formulate guidelines, and

c) conservation of threatened species of fauna, increasing their rate of production, maintaining their original habitat, determining bag limits, controlling population in relation to the camping capacity of the land and banning indiscriminate or destructive means of hunting or catching (*Ibid.*, Section 29).

b) Environmental Impact Analysis

The creation of reserves may protect the environmental quality of certain sensitive areas. An enclave approach which says in essence, "do what you like so long as it doesn't affect these specific lands" is unlikely, however, to maintain or improve environmental quality on a broad scale. Instead, what is needed is an approach which turns the environmental focus upon specific development decisions. For this purpose, two project-specific alternatives present themselves. The first of these is the environmental impact analysis.

Today, project-specific environmental impact analysis ("EIA") is a relatively routine part of decision-making in many of the more developed countries. The routine performance of such analysis, however, belies the fact that EIA is a relatively recent phenomenon. Indeed, the cornerstone of EIA was not laid until 1969 with passage of the United States National Environmental Policy Act ("NEPA") [57/]. In part, NEPA was a response to mounting public concern that environmental considerations had been avoided in the planning of major public works projects. In part it was also a response to a less well-defined shift in values among the public who began to focus more attention upon the quality of life and the things which contribute to it. The depth of this feeling was, in fact demonstrated by the speed with which virtually all of the states of the United States and many of the countries of Europe passed environmental impact legislation of their own within a few years of the enactment of NEPA [58/].

57/ Public Law 91-190, Title 42 United States Code, section 4321 *et. seq.*; 83 Stat 852.

58/ See, e.g., Yost, *NEPA's Progeny : State Environmental Policy Acts* 3 Environment Law Reporter 50090 (1973).

The heart of the environmental legislation typified by NEPA is the requirement that government - before it commences the construction of any major work which may significantly affect the human environment - must prepare a statement which focusses upon environmental issues. These statements, now commonly referred to as environmental impact reports, are generally required to discuss in detail the following :

(i) the environmental impact of the proposed action,

(ii) mitigation measures which will reduce or eliminate adverse environmental impacts of the proposed action;

(iii) any adverse environmental effects which cannot be avoided should the proposal be implemented;

(iv) alternatives to the proposed action;

(v) the relationship between local short-term uses of man's environment and the maintenance and enhancement of long-term productivity;

(vi) any significant irreversible environmental changes or committment of resources which would be involved in the proposed action should it be implemented 59/.

In general, these requirements have prompted government to give greater thought to the environmental effects of their actions before those actions result in the implementation of projects that have significant adverse environmental consequences. Where a particular environmental impact law provides (or has been interpreted by the courts to provide) standing for

---

59/ See, e.g., NEPA para. 102, 42 USC para. 4332 (c); California Environmental Quality Act, Public Resources Code, Section 21100.

citizens to challenge the sufficiency of the government's analysis, the tendency by government to avoid its environmental responsibilities has been reduced. This is not to say that environmentally damaging projects are no longer approved and constructed in the venues which have such laws. They are, and probably will continue to be constructed where there is sufficient political muscle to propel them forward despite the consequences. Just as certainly, however, well drafted environmental impact legislation has caused government to re-think and replan some harmful projects. It has also, in general, raised the threshold of political power needed to push a project through despite its environmental problems.

Notwithstanding the substantial and unarguable benefits which accrue from environmental impact analysis, there are several things which should be considered before EIA is given wholesale application to the process of development in the rural sector of developing countries. First, is the matter of time. Environmental impact analysis is slow. Indeed, it succeeds in part by purposely slowing the development process down so that the decision maker will have the time to consider the environmental cost of the activity under review. Frequently, however, the approach to land development in developing countries has been one of "full-speed ahead". Is then the concept of EIA compatible with the desires of decision-makers ? The answer probably is yes, in most cases. First, it is possible to streamline the EIA process. Much of the delay attributable to EIA has occured at the back-end of the process in the form of litigation brought by individuals challenging the adequacy of a particular EIA in the light of statutory requirements [60/]. Certainly such challenges may produce benefits - generally in the form of keeping the decision maker honest in his evaluations. If public participation is increased at the front end of the process, before the EIR is written, however, the beneficial effect of subsequent litigation becomes more marginal and, may be dispensible.

60/ By court decision those challenges have been limited usually to challenges to the procedural adequacy of the EIR; courts generally have been unwilling to second guess an EIR's conclusions about environmental impact.

Second, the concept of EIA is likely to be compatible with the desires of decision-makers in developing countries for the simple reason that such people, themselves, are becoming more and more sophisticiated about the detriments as well as the benefits of development. Increasingly rare are the decision-makers who desire development even at the cost of their country's social, cultural and environmental amenities. Thus, the lawyer or planner may find a surpringly receptive audience if the concept is presented.

Somewhat less favor may be shown, however, to the notion of extensive public participation in the process of EIA. Technocrats have an unfortunate tendency to view members of the public who seek a role in the development process as "meddlers". The technocrats in developing countries are, regrettably, no exception. Thus, to avoid creating opposition to the effort to introduce environmental concerns into the land development process, careful limits upon the frequency and depth of public participation may have to be drawn. It should be stressed, however, that the EIA process works best when the public participates. The "meddlers" in fact tend to be far outnumbered by those with a genuine concern over the potential impact of a project on their environment. Accordingly, some public participation is essential, and efforts to turn EIA into a process that is solely of, by and for technical officials should be resisted.

c) Regulatory Control of Environmental Impacts

Finally, government policies regarding environmental protection may be implemented through a regulatory system which limits the environmental impact of development through permit and license controls. Depending upon how they are designed, these controls may regulate either the direct or secondary impacts of development.

Direct impacts are those which arise from the immediate development, itself. Visual impact, noise pollution and waste discharges into the air and water from grading, construction, pesticide application and manufacturing, are all direct impacts that can be controlled through permits which condition the right to carry on the activity upon compliance with permit terms. Secondary impacts are those which do not necessarily arise from the development activity itself but which, on the other hand, would not exist "but for" the development. Development which attracts workers who collectively deplete available water supplies thus produces a secondary impact. Development which manufactures products (such as pesticides) whose use within the country has adverse environmental consequences generates a secondary impact. Similarly development whose demand for inputs (such as electricity) generates additional development with adverse environmental consequences, produces a secondary impact.

In such cases, the environmental provisions of land use legislation have an important role to play. First, they can give legal recognition to the fact the development may generate secondary environmental consequences. Recognizing the existence of a problem, after all, constitutes the first step in solving it. Second, such provisions provide the means for attributing legal responsibility for secondary consequences to the development which has, in fact, generated those consequences. Thus, if the development of a manufacturing or processing operation creates a demand for energy that necessitates the construction of new energy facilities (a hydropower project for example) those consequences can (indeed, must) legally be considered part of the <u>initial</u> development and thus put into the balance in determining whether the benefits of that project outweight its costs. Moreover, if the initial development is legally linked to the secondary impacts which are generated, there then exists a legal basis for conditioning approval of the initial development upon the obligation to undertake measures which are designed to mitigate or eliminate secondary impacts. Indeed, <u>unless</u> such an obligation is legally established, the initial developer may well succeed in shifting certain of the costs ("externalizing" the costs, in economic parlance) of his development to the public.

10. Government Priorities Respecting the Use of Land

A particular government may also emphasize certain "priorities" respecting the development of land. Typically, these will favor one particular use from among several alternative uses of the same parcel of land and, in effect, amount to an additional statement of government policy.

The spectrum of potential government priorities regarding the use of land is, of course, considerable. Moreover, the land development priorities which any particular government employs may vary considerably from country to country (or even region to region) according to the specific political, social, geographic and economic circumstances which exist. Nevertheless, it is possible to identify some of the more obvious priorities which should be explored by the lawyer or planner concerned with land development legislation.

a) Export/Staple Crop Priorities

One decision which government may make in planning the development of land is whether to give priority to the production of export crops or to staple crops intended for domestic consumption. If the land in issue possesses attributes which may give certain crops a comparative advantage on world markets, then a decision to give priority to growing crops for the export market may well be a means of raising foreign exchange which can be used to gain access to needed goods and services not otherwise available within the country. On the other hand, priority for staple crops may expand domestic food production and thus decrease the need to import foodstuffs thus decreasing the need for foreign exchange to purchase such commodities.

If government has expressed the desire for a legislative statement of such a priority - or if it is determined that such a priority is useful for development purposes and should therefore be legislatively expressed - it is worth considering the inclusion in land development legislation of a guideline which steers agricultural development toward particular crops (export or domestic) 61/.

b) Water Development Priorities

An obvious limitation upon land development may be the indadequacy of existing water supplies. Thus, economic development may include increasing the availability of surplus water 62/ so as to satisfy new consumptive uses. Precisely how the quantity of surplus water will be increased, however, may well be the subject of legislative language which establishes a priority in this regard.

Large scale water development works are frequently expensive, as well as being socially and environmentally disruptive 63/. On the other hand, water conservation actions - including the recycling and re-use of wastewater for agricultural purposes - can produce similar increases in water supplies at a fraction of the economic and social cost 64/. Thus, it may be

---

61/ Such guideline, for instance, might state that to further the national interest, preference will be given to land development schemes which will result in the growing of staple (or export) crops, other factors being equal.

62/ Surplus water is simply the quantity found in a water supply source (such as a river, or an acquifer) at any point in time, which is en excess of the reasonable needs of water users already making beneficial use of water.

63/ On the other hand, of course, they may create jobs (at least during the period of construction) and produce other benefits such as power production or increased recreational opportunities.

64/ Conceededly, water conservation measures may be difficult to enforce without a strong administrative infrastructure - something which may be lacking in a developing country.

appropriate for the government to consider the creation of a priority scheme which will express a preference for water conservation measures rather than water development works, where it can be established that similar increases in the quantity of available surplus water will result from each alternative.

c) Agricultural/Urban Development Priorities

The earlier discussion of a policy for the preservation of prime agricultural land leads to consideration of whether the government has - or should have - a policy of giving priority to developments which maintain the agricultural use of land located at the urban/rural interface. Inevitably governments will be confronted with choices regarding the development of such lands. If a priority favoring agrarian development is legislatively expressed, the loss of valuable farmland may be slowed. This is so, since decision-makers will be obliged to consider whether the benefits of a proposed commercial or industrial development are so significant that the development should proceed notwithstanding the expressed agrarian priority.

At the same time, however, an expression of priority for agrarian development would not act as an insurmontable barrier to commercial or industrial development. It is, after all, a statement of priority; not a moratorium on non-agrarian development. In appropriate cases, where the benefits of a particular non-agrarian development are clear, the priority would not bar the proponents of the development from proceeding.

d) Agricultural/Wildlife Priorities

The need to protect resources located at the margin of development also suggests consideration of a legislatively expressed priority concerning agriculture and wildlife. The expansion of agricultural activities frequently results in a reduction of habitat for wildlife species. Concomitantly, a reduction in habitat translates to a reduction in the number of species making use of the habitat. The result is that expanded agricultural activities often equate with declines in the number of wild creatures.

Unfortunately, in many developing countries, there may be no one to advocate the needs of wildlife - particularly in the face of demands for expanded food production. The loss of the nation's wildlife heritage, however, is a high price to pay for expanded food production capabilities; especially if intelligent planning could produce similar productivity gains at a greatly reduced wildlife cost. Accordingly, it may be appropriate to propose a government statement of policy expressed in terms of a priority given to wildlife preservation and enhancement. This is not to suggest that an entire country or region should be turned into an enormous national park at the expense of its human inhabitants. It is important to draw the attention of land use decision-makers, however, to the significance of certain critical habitats, the dangers of over-exploitation and the fact that the land developer, no less than the hunter, can be responsible for direct, adverse impacts to wildlife. By means of appropriate limitations as to geography and species, moreover, the effect of a proposed wildlife priority can be tailored to conform to the precise circumstances at hand and thus reduce the impact upon agrarian development to the minimum necessary for responsible wildlife management.

e) Agriculture/Forestry Priorities

A final matter of government policy which may exist in the form of a priority, concerns the relative development of agricultural and forestry lands. Not infrequently, this involves the clearing of forested lands. Moreover, government itself may seek to expand farmland by encouraging the clearing of forested terrain. As a result, not only may water supplies be threatened by a loss of watershed, or by pollution, but necessary supplies of fuel for cooking may be put in jeopardy.

Given the pressures already faced by forested land, it may be appropriate to propose legislative assistance in the form of a priority for development that will enhance, or at least preserve, forest lands. Thus, decision-makers would not only be obliged to enquire about forestry impacts, they would be obliged as well to select the least damaging alternative. Moreover, the expression of such a priority would also tend to provide decision makers with the authority to condition agricultural developments upon reforestation efforts.

In sum, a forestry priority - like the other priorities mentioned - is a means of guiding the development process in order to give the individuals making decisions about land use the opportunity (as well as the responsibility) to consider the consequences of their actions. Further, since such a priority is also an expression of national policy, it serves to arm the decision-maker with the legal authority to conform land development to the national will and to stop (by failing to approve or by more affirmative measures) proposed developments which do not conform or cannot be conformed.

CHAPTER III - EVALUATING THE EXISTING LAND USE DECISION-MAKING STRUCTURE

Any effort to improve the way in which decisions about the use of land are made presupposes an undertanding of how existing land use decisions making procedures operates. On a more subtle level, a thorough study of the existing decision-making process is also apt to reveal something of the nature of the policial forces at work in the process. At heart, an effort to change the way decisions about land are made, is a political effort. Thus, disclosure of the identity of the persons or government agencies who hold the power to make - or block - land use decisions may reveal a kind of topographical map which depicts the political turf likely to be defended against efforts to change the way in which land use decisions are reached. If these political forces are unknown they may be ignored, or worse, unconsciously transgressed, with potentially fatal consequences to the reform effort. If, on the other hand, such forces are relatively well understood, they may even be incorporated into the reform effort, thus perhaps converting a potential political adversary into a supporter

As was the case with government policies and priorities, the land use decision making process which exists, in fact, may differ considerably from that which is supposed to exist as a result of various legal pronouncements on the subject of land use. Thus, it may be necessary to look beyond the statutory risks in order to produce an accurate map of the existing decision-making process. One example -chosen not because it is unique, but rather because it is typical - should suffice to make the point.

In the Sudan, the Unregistered Lands Act (Act No. 3 of 1970) provides that all unregistered land (more than 90 percent of all land in the Sudan) is :

> "... the property of the Government and shall be deemed to have been registered as such, as if the provisions of the Land Settlement and Registration Act have been duly complied with 65/."

65/ The Land Settlement and Registration Act referred to, dates from 1925 and provides for the registration of land in the name of particular owners, as well as for the preservation and recording of servitudes and other rights of use not amounting to ownership.

In fact, however, the vesting of title to land in "the Government" does little to explain the reality of how land use determinations are made for such lands. In fact, "the Government" - meaning the Central Government in Khartoum - plays a largely secondary role in deciding the use to be made of particular acreage. Under the law, no specific agency of the Government has been charged with the responsibility of managing government land. In practice until 1980, however, a process developed of government agencies referring their project proposals to the relevant provincial government for a determination of the existence of competing land use claims. If the agency received a certificate that competing claims were few or none, it would proceed to survey and demarcate the land, effectively "claiming" it as against other government agencies. Where there were competing claims, the agency might take the land and exclude claimed areas, incorporate users in its scheme, or compensate them. According to some sources, provincial (now regional) governments frustrated some central government plans by falsely claiming that too many other rights existed in the area [66/]. They also proceeded to allocate land on their own.

To attempt to deal with this situation, the Central Government has adopted the Encouragement of Investment Act which expressly gives the power to "allot" land to the Central Ministry of Finance [67/]. In practice, however, this power has not been directly exercised by the Ministry. Indeed, in practice, even more responsibility is given to local government and with less legal basis for doing so. Although the Investment Act empowers the Ministry of Finance to "allot" land to investors (section 11), the Ministry of Agriculture, in practice, allots land in a preliminary procedure and the land it allots is normally that which is assigned for the purpose by relevant <u>regional</u> authorities who communicate their choice of land

---

66/ See Wilkinson and Christy, "Review of Agricultural Legislation in the Sudan"' TCP/SUD/2210, Rome, 1983.

67/ Encouragement of Investment Act, 19080, sec. 11.

to the central agriculture ministry. In other words, regional responsibility is not limited to approval of a choice of investments, but actually extends to land selection 68/. In the end, the allotment is confirmed by the Ministry of Finance's approval of the project; thus, in a sense it could be said that the whole process concludes consistently with the Act. Quite clearly, however, the Act does not define the parameters process as they exist in practice.

The lessons to be drawn from the above example are relatively simple. First, the actual practice of decision making about land can diverse significantly from the scheme set forth in pertinent legislation. Second, in order to accurately determine the nature of the process, in practice, it is essential to investigate beyond the code books by talking to the people who actually participate in the process. Only in that way is it likely that a true picture of the political forces at work in the process will be composed. If such an investigation is undertaken, we believe it should attempt to form as complete a picture as possible about the following elements of the actual decision-making process :

1. who are the relevant players (individuals and institutions) and at what level do they participate ?

2. what connections exist between players on the same level or on different levels ?

3. What form does the process take and what factors influence the decision ?

4. To what extent is the public included within the decision-making process and to what extent are the land use decisions generated by the process made subject to review ? and

---

68/ Frequently, it also happens in practice that particular land is requested by the investor.

5. Is there practical and substantial monitoring and enforcement of the decisions generated by the process ?

In the remaining portion of this chapter we shall elaborate upon the relevancy of the enumerated elements.

1. The Players and the Level of their Participation

Decisions about the use of land are made by people. Determining who and where those people are is one way of beginning to form a picture of the system of decision-making that exists in practice.

Beginning at the lowest level, it is obvious that individual users will make decisions about particular parcels of land. Indeed, even if land use occurs in accordance with a central, regional or even local plan of same sort, it is unlikely that such a plan will be sufficiently detailed to eliminate all discretionary decisions by the individual farmer or other user. Thus, it is almost certain that individual users will form a significant part of any system of decision making about land.

Skipping to the highest level, it is also likely that a particular country will have some kind of central plan that relates to land use. The detail found in such a plan will vary considerably from venue to venue with it consisting, in some instances, of little more than a 3 or 5 or 10 year master plan for growth. More than likely such a plan will be approved at a very high level - usually the ministerial level. Further, the plan is likely to have technical input from the ministries whose ministers sit in a judgmental capacity over the plan. Typically, preparation of such a central plan is not entrusted to the Ministry of Agriculture. Rather, technical control is often exercised by a Ministry of Planning or Finance, with Agriculture given an advisory role similar to that accorded to a variety of other sectoral ministries.

On the other hand, rather than producing a general master plan for economic growth, the central government may have made provision for a relatively detailed plan that focusses specifically upon the subject of land use; either country-wide, by region or by tribal or other sub-classification 69/. Or, the central government may in fact be involved with land use planning through legislation which is directed at land consolidation 70/, land reform 71/ or soil conservation 72/. Under the terms of such legislation the Government is likely to have established a central board or authority composed of high level technical (as opposed to ministerial) officials and empowered to engage in activities which may range from the adoption of general land use guidelines, to the review of local or regionally prepared plans or the actual demarcation of planning areas and issuance of land use permits.

69/ See, for example the Botswana, Town and Country Planning Act (Act No. 11 of 1977); the Town and Country Planning Act of Malaysia (Act No. 172 of 1976); the Thailand Land Development Act (B.E. 2526), and the Land Act of Lesotho (Act No. 17 of 1979).

70/ See, for instance, sec. 26 of the Land Consolidation Law of Cyprus (No. 24 of 1969) and sec. 2 of Land Consolidation Authority Annual Report, 1979.

71/ The Land Reform Act of Peru (Decreto-Ley No. 17.716 of 1969), for example provides for the carrying out of land reform under a system of zones (Title IV) and authorizes re-allocation of land, livestock, crops, installations and equipment in such zones to agricultural firms (cooperatives) representing a social interest (Title VI). Small scale farmers, among others moreover, are entitled to priority for the allocation of lands they are working and enjoy preference for the grant of technical and credit assistance (Titles VI and VII).

72/ The Rwanda Soil Conservation Law (Act No. 11/82 relative to soil protection, conservation and use (1982), for example sets forth detailed requirements concerning farming practices, reforestation and the practice of shifting cultivation.

Regarding such central boards or authorities, several questions are worth asking. First, it should be enquired whether the high level technical membership designated by law actually attends the meetings of the board or authority or, instead, delegates responsibility to subordinates. In fact, such delegation of responsibility occurs frequently and is not, per se, something to be criticized. A subordinate department head may not only have more time than a director-general to attend regular planning meetings but may also, in fact, be better qualified to make the technical judgments that contribute to a final land-use decision. Problems can arise, however, if the subordinate delegee, in fact, lacks the authority to speak on behalf of his or her ministry, or if the delegation rotates among a variety of people according to who happens to be available for duty. Regular attendance by the same person of sufficient rank to speak on behalf of a ministry is, in practice, essential to rational, consistent decision-making.

A second question to ask regarding the various land use related boards and authorities established at the central level is whether a) they actually exist and b) whether they actually perform all of their legal responsibilities. With surprising frequency, competently drafted, detailed legislation exists but has not been implemented. Funding difficulties and manpower shortages instead preclude the formation or operation of legally authorized boards and thus defeat the government's good intentions.

Typically, sub-national officials are also involved in land use decision-making, often at a variety of levels. In a federal system, for example, it is not unusual to find a state-level planning committee which coordinates the function of local planning authorities within that state 73/. Similarly, where there is an emphasis upon the regionalization of government affairs, the central government may operate in each region through

---

73/ An example of precisely this sort of structure is found in the Town and Country Planning Act of Malaysia (Act No. 172 of 1976).

nominally central government staff who have been secunded to the region and who, in fact, bring a regional perspective to planning and other government affairs 74/. Further, there may be instances where geographic areas in particular need of planning do not fit neatly within the boundaries of a state, region or even municipality. In response, the existing system may include "planning areas" over which the functions of a central board have been delegated to a special planning authority 75/.

Finally, it is important to recognize that land use decisions inevitably have to be implemented at the local level. Are local officials involved ? Do they participate by virtue of statutory provisions authorizing their involvement, or informally ? Quite likely, these may be some of the most difficult questions to answer, since local people are not easy for the consultant to reach 76/. However, because, local officials and local land users are the persons who can make or break the government's land use programme, it is worth the considerable effort involved to determined whether and to what extent such people participate in planning the use of land.

73/ An example of precisely this sort of structure is found in the Town and Country Planning Act of Malaysia (Act No. 172 of 1976).

74/ Such a system, for example, is used throughout most of the Sudan.

75/ Such a system of planning areas has been established in Botswana by the Town and Country Planning Act (Act No. 11 of 1977) and implemented through the Town and Country Planning (Declaration of Planning Areas) Order, 1980.

76/ We have, frankly, noticed a tendency for central government level officials to neglect arranging contacts between consultants and local types. In part, this may be due to the fact that such officials themselves have little contact with the locals.

2. <u>What connections exist between participants in the land use decision-making process on one level and between participants on different levels</u> ?

Another question related to the process of making decisions about the use of land, concerns the nature of the connections which exist between people involved in the process. Between people on the same level, such connections can be viewed as horizontal. Does the Minister of Planning (or Finance) talk with the Minister of Agriculture about decisions concerning the use of agrarian land ? Does he talk to the Minister of Health about decisions affecting such land, or affecting agrarian people ? Do technical counterparts at the various central ministries meet and confer ? At the regional level ? What connections are there among people at the local level ?

Equally important, are there vertical connections between persons involved in the process of land use decision-making on different levels and, if so, in what direction does information and responsibility flow ? Is the existing system a top/down one where decisions are made at the central level without the participation of sub-national people who are expected simply to implement what they are told ? Or is there a bottom/up system where initial decisions (or plans) are constructed at the sub-national level and sent to the central government for harmonization and inclusion in a long-term economic plan ? Or is there instead, some combination of the above, with information flowing back and forth and decisions being made at the sub-national level in accordance with detailed guidelines and close central monitoring or at the central level with frequent sub-national input. In this regard, it is worth remembering that even a fully operational central land use board or authority is likely to have limited importance, if it is not linked in some manner to regional, state or local officials. This is so since, poor communications, thin staffing, impassable roads and the other elements of weak infrastructure all act to thwart the planning, implementation and enforcement efforts of central officials. Local politics and regionalist tendencies may be an additional aggravating factor. As a consequence, some countries have acted to include people from the regional, state or local levels in the land use planning process at the central level.

In essence, the questions about horizontal and vertical connections are political questions which explore the character of the governmental framework that exists in a particular country. Because the questions are political, the answers are likely to be a reflection of political circumstances which will, of course, vary from country to country. Accordingly, it is difficult to predict whether there will be horizontal and vertical contacts and, if so, how extensive and useful those contacts will be. A centrally planned economy, for example, is unlikely to have many vertical connections which feed the land use planning process with information from the bottom-up. While there may be vertical connections, they will more than likely exist to promote a one-way flow of information from the top-down. Similarly, if one central or regional ministry is directed by an extremely powerful minister at the political level (or Director-General at the technical level) who has an interest in land use planning, the horizontal contacts with other ministries may be minimal [77/]. Or, if a particular ministry or department is run by a relatively weak minister or director, that ministry (or Department) may have relatively few connections with the process of land use planning, notwithstanding its importance to that process.

3. What Form does the Existing Land-Use Planning Process Take and What Factors Influence the Decision ?

After the participants in the existing land use planning process have been located and the connections which exist between and among them have been disclosed, it is important to ascertain how the process actually operates and what factors influence the ultimate decision.

The manner in which the decision making-process operates will vary considerably according to the jurisdiction under study. There may, however, be certain forms against which a particular decision-making process can be compared.

77/ Or, for similar reasons, such connections could be maximal - if the minister or director is interested in exercising this power to produce a balanced process of decision-making.

In some regions, South-East Asia being one, for example, decison-making at both the technical and political levels tends to proceed by way of consensus. Although public confrontations between citizens and officials in an organized hearing context may be relatively rare 78/, an administrative decision to proceed with he development of land or water resources is normally not taken until a consensus about the propriety of the decision is reached among interested government departments and ministries. Precisely how each such department or ministry reaches its own decision is not detailed in the statutory law. Practice, however, suggests that such decision may be the product of contacts by central ministry or department officials not only with other central officials, but also with state, regional or local officials and with interested members of the public who may be beneficially or detrimentally affected if the proposed decision is implemented 79/. Thus,

---

78/ The idea of public hearings along the lines of a town meeting appears to be a western concept that has not been readily adopted in other parts of the world. The absence of public hearings, however, does not *per se* mark a particular land use decision-making process as abnormally closed and secretive, especially when opposition may be expressed in other forms. For instance, neither the Land Development Act of Thailand (B.E. 2526), the Town and Country Planning act of Malaysia (Act No. 172 of 1976) nor the Indonesian Basic Regulations on Agrarian Principles (Act No. 5 of 1960) contain requirements for public hearings at which members of the public - particularly those adversely affected by a specific proposed land use decision - may state their views and cross - examine proponents of the proposed decisions. In all three countries, however, the tendency is to proceed to a decision through a process of consensus; an approach which tends to inject a relatively wide diversity of opinion into the proceedings.

79/ Such extra-legal contacts are especially numerous in a federally administered multi-racial and egalitarian society such as Malaysia, for example and where the state level of government is stron, when there is a tradition of contact between the governors and the governed.

even though a public hearing requirement does not exist, a relatively wide variety of views, including perhaps the views of interested citizens, may nonetheless be fed into the decision-making process.

This is not to suggest, of course, that all land use decision-making processes are formally or informally set up to include a diversity of views and opinions. Many are not. Instead, decisions about the use of land may be made by fiat with little input from the sub-national level, with little public participation, with few if any guidelines and with almost no dissenting views expressed. And such a "process" - if it can be called that - may produce land use decisions. Whether those decisions actually achieve government policies and objectives; indeed, whether they are even implemented at the user level, is another question, however. If decisions are truly made in a vacuum, the likelihood of their implementation is probably inversely related to the distance the decision-maker resides from the site involved.

In fact, however, the probability of land use decisions being made in a complete vacuum in an authoritarian setting is relatively small. Some technical or social input is likely to creep into the process of decision-making no matter how tightly controlled it is at the top. In these circumstances, it is especially important to discover these inputs and learn how they are fed into the process, since any effort to liberalize the process is more likely to succeed if it utilizes known personnel and proceeds along already established (even if feeble) lines.

A second set of questions to ask about the working of any existing land use decision making process concerns the existence of norms used in reaching decisions about how to use land. Has the government (national, regional or local) established any guidelines which influence the process or direct the outcome when the decision maker is faced with alternatives ? Are there statutory objectives which reflect the government's land-related social and economic policies and priorities (see Chapter II, above) and how do those objectives fit into the process ? On the other hand, are there extra-legal practices which, through frequency of occurrence, have become norms that influence the land development process ? For instance, is there a practice of lobbying or influence pedaling ? Of bribery ? If so, how pervasive is it and does it produce side benefits to the larger public interest ? Have reform measures previously been tried and why did they not succeed ? What is the government's current prevailing attitude about such practices and about measures intended to effect reform ?

Obviously, some of the above issues will have to be treated delicately and approached very carefully. On the other hand, if a true picture of the existing situation is sought, such issues should be explored.

4. To What Extent is the Public Included Within the Decision-Making Process and to What Extent are Decisions Generated by the Process Made Subject to Review ?

We have heretofore discussed the matter of public involvement in the land use decision-making process. If suffices to say that public involvement relates closely to public acceptance and, ultimately, effective implementation by the public of decisions yielded by the land development process. Accordingly, it is useful to examine how and to what extent the existing land use decision-making process involves the public.

For this purpose, it is probably most convenient to begin with an examination of existing legislation. Occasionally, such an examination will disclose statutory provisions which formally grant a right to members of the public to voice their views about a proposed land use decision. Typically, the right to be heard relates to the issuance of a licence or permit concerning the use of land - to construct a building, make a diversion of water, discharge waste or harvest timber 80/. Occasionally, however, the public may

---

80/ See, for example, the Town and Country Planning Act (Act No. 172 of 1976) Malaysia; the Agriculture Act of Kenya, sec. 77 (Act 8 of 1955); Botswana, Town and Country Planning Order (1980), sec. 6(3); Belize Land Utilization Ordinance (1981), sec. 10.

be given the opportunity to comment upon even more generalized land use schemes; for example, the establishment of watershed protection areas, land reform zones or water use plans which affect customary or privately held lands 81/. It is also possible that public input to the land use decision-making process exists irrespective of formal authorization in a law. Because of its fundamental character, land use is likely to be the subject of discussion at the village level. If that discussion reveals local opposition to a particular decision involving local lands, such opposition probably will be expressed through some channel to the decision maker.

Whether the channel of public input is tribal or political or follows some other form, its disclosure is important since, if it works to promote public participation, it may be possible to formalize the channel of communication through the drafting of a land use development law. Indeed, even a government otherwise resistant to public participation in the decision-making process 82/ may have no objection to a statutory provision which simply formalizes a means of communication that already exists.

The question of public participation relates to involvement in the making of a land use decision. A connected issue concerns public involvement after the decision is made and is generally dealt with under the rubric of "appeals". More specifically, it is useful to investigate 1) whether land use decisions are subject to appeal and by whom; 2) to whom the appeal is made; and 3) what is the scope of review of such appeals as are allowed.

81/ See, e.g. the proposed Samoa Water Resources Act (1985), sec. 15 (public comment on effect of water works on customary and privately held land); Proposed Tonga Water Resources Act (1985), sec. 59 (public comment on proposed watershed protection areas); Peru Land Reform Act (1969), Title IV (public comment on government declaration of land reform zone).

82/ It is an unfortunate truism that many technical officials the world-over view lay people who are concerned about government decisions affecting basic natural resources, as "intermeddlers".

Generally, if appeals are authorized, they are limited to persons who are "aggrieved" by a particular governmental decision 83/. Exactly who is an "aggrieved" person may be subject to some dispute, however. Almost certainly the term would include an applicant for a permit or license or someone whose land is directly affected by a land use decision. Does it include someone who is "interested" albeit not directly affected by such a decision; e.g. a tribal or environmental group ? Probably the statute is unclear and it may be necessary to consult relevant court decisions or evaluate the prevailing administrative practice to ascertain the answer.

A second issue involves the question to whom is the appeal to be made. The answer generally falls into one of two categories, one of which involves review by a disinterested third party and one of which does not. In many cases, the only review of an appeal raised by an aggrieved person is by the minister whose ministry has rendered the challenged decision 84/. Such an "in-house" appeal necessarily raises the question of the fundamental fairness of the review accorded to the appellant. While it may be more administratively convenient and avoid court congestion, an in-house review clearly includes the risk that the review will, in fact, be made (or at least heavily influenced) by the same officials who rendered the challenged decision in the first place. Thus, a careful evaluation of the equity accorded to appellants should be made in such circumstances.

83/ See, e.g., sec. 14, the Tribal Land Act of Botswana (1970); sec. 16, The Land Act of Lesotho (1979); sec. 35, Environmental Quality Act of Malaysia (1974); sec. 52, the Agriculture Act of Kenya (1955); and sec. 20, the Land Consolidation Law of Cyprus (1969).

84/ Of the legislation cited in the previous footnote, for example, both the Botswana Tribal Land Act and the Agriculture Act of Kenya provide for appeals to the Minister or the Ministry making the challenged decision. In each case, the Minister's decision is final.

The second category of appeals involves those which are made to more disintersted parties such as a review board 85/ or the courts 86/. Theoretically at least, such review is more independent. Whether it is in fact independent, however, depends largely upon the scope of review - the third major issue to be explored in any analysis of appeal rights.

If the entity reviewing an appeal of a land use decision has the power to re-weigh the evidence previously presented to the administrative agency whose decision has been appealed, then it is considered to be exercising its "independent judgment" on the matter. Generally, reviewing bodies which employ an "independent judgment test" are less confined by the rulings of a lower administrative body and will uphold the decision of such or lesser body only if it (the reviewer) would have made the same decision in light of all the evidence. Generally too, reviewing bodies in such circumstances have the power to take new evidence beyond that presented to the lower administrative body whose decison has been appealed. With such independent reviewing bodies, the trade-off for independence is that, ultimately, a technical decision involving complicated alternative choices regarding land will not be made by an expert technical body; but rather, by an inexpert reviewing body such as a court.

Partly as result of the foregoing trade-off, some legislation prescribes a narrower scope of review by the reviewer. Generally such review is described by the phrase "substantial evidence". In effect this means that the scope of review will be limited to a determination of whether there is any substantial evidence in the administrative record to support the decision of

---

85/ In Lesotho an appeal of a decision of a Land Committee is, for example, made to the next highest Land Committee. Land Act, Sec. 16. In Malaysia, any appeal under the Environmental Quality Act is to an Appeal Board (Sec. 35).

86/ Under recently drafted legislation for Samoa and Tonga, appeals involving land included within a watershed protection zone (which inclusion comes with a variety of land use restrictions) is to a court of competent jurisdiction. Proposed Samoa Water Resources Act, sec. 63; proposed Tonga Water Act, Sec. 65.

the administrative body being appealed. If there is, then the reviewer must affirm that decision even if the reviewer would have reached a different result in the first instance. If there is not, the reviewer vacates the decision and sends it back to the reviewing body to reconsider in light of the reviewer's opinion. The advantage of such limited review is two-fold. First, it respects the presumed technical expertise of the administrative body making the land-use decision. Second, it provides for a disinterested review of that decision and, in cases where the decision is arbitrary (i.e., unsupported by any substantial evidence), allows for a reversal.

5. Monitoring and Enforcement of Decisions Generated by the Land Use Process

Finally, in the course of evaluating the existing land use decision making structure, it is important to determine whether provision is made for the monitoring of compliance with land use decisions and what, if any, enforcement measures exist to prevent non-compliance.

Even if there is a well planned decision making structure with numerous horizontal and vertical connections,thoughtful guidelines and objectives, broad provisions for useful public participation and a sensible appeal mechanism, the structure is virtually useless if land users ignore the decisions it generates. Accordingly, to ensure integrety, there should exist some means of uncovering non-compliance and sufficient authority to terminate non-compliance when it is found.

Frankly, in our experience, most existing natural resources legislation is weak in this area. Generally speaking, a monitoring mechanism has not found its way into most laws. Moreover, if non-compliance with a permit or license or prohibition is somehow discovered, most legislation provides for a relatively unsophisticated response - almost always a fine or imprisonment. This is not to say, of course, that compliance monitoring never occurs. It frequently does; however, it is often more a matter of happenstance than the result of any regular, systematic programme. Someone travelling a public thoroughfare, for instance, sees unusual activity on adjacent land and reports the matter to someone else who may or may not follow it up.

Moreover, the informal compliance monitoring which may occur is not only haphazard in its timing, it also tends to be very limited in its scope. If no legal provision is made for a monitoring programme, then almost certainly there is inadequate authority for governmental officials to gain access to private property or undertake sampling or other technical measures to determine compliance. Indeed, the problem of public officials gaining access to private property is one which arises again and again. Because of these problems the not too surprising result is that the informal compliance monitoring which does exist, occurs mostly in areas which can be seen from public lands. If the activity occurs on private land, out of sight, behind a fence or a land contour, it probably will not be monitored.

Similarly, the enforcement remedies which exist should be evaluated for their practicality. If existing law provides for a draconian penalty (criminal or civil) in the event of a violation of a government decision regarding land, the chances are it will not be enforced. Not only might attempted enforcement subject the enforcing official (who almost certainly lives in the same community) to physical reprisal or social obloquy, it would also likely result in another needy family being added to an already existing burden on the state.

Thus, it is useful to determine whether there are non-statutory enforcement measures which can be applied to restrain those who seek to evade the decisions of the government (or the local community) respecting the use of land. Where statutory enforcement measures are draconian, the chances are that such other measures exist; quite possibly in the form of customary laws or practices. The chances also are that if such measures are a part of customary practice, they have been accepted at the land user level and thus tend to accomplish their purpose. The field of customary practice is an enormous and complicated one that is largely beyond the scope of this work. It bears emphasis, however, that customary practices should _always_ be considered, _occasionally_ embraced and _never_ ignored. That is especially true regarding to measures intended to achieve compliance with decisions generated by the land use structure. If a customary enforcement practice works, it is worth thinking about including the practice as part of an effort to statutorily rationalize the land use decision making process.

CHAPTER IV - INFLUENCE OF EXISTING LAND TENURE PATTERNS AND CUSTOMARY PRACTICES ON THE LAND USE DECISION-MAKING PROCESS

Inevitably, governmental decisions about the use of land will intersect existing patterns of land tenure. Such decisions may also encounter claims of use or possession based upon custom, if an active system of customary land law exists - as it does in many African countries. Whether these points of intersection will be benign or confrontational and whether it will be the pattern of land tenure or the governmental decision which gives way if there is a confrontation, depends upon a variety of factors. Among them are issues of who owns the land in a legal sense; who possesses or controls the land in fact, and the extent to which customary rights are respected by and integrated into the existing system of law. In this chapter, we shall briefly explore the potential influence of each of these factors upon the process of making decisions about the use of land.

1. Who Owns the Land in a Legal Sense ?

Land use decisions which promote or restrict development on land that is government owned will likely have legal, economic and political consequences substantially different from decisions affecting privately owned land. Among other things, it is the private ownership of land in the legal sense [87/] which may give the individual a legal right to resist a government taking - or even government

87/ By "ownership of land in the legal sense" we mean ownership under color of law.

regulation of the use of land 88/ - unless compensation is paid by the Government for its interference with the private right of ownership. Thus, private ownership can serve as a legal impediment to government decision-making about the use of land.

For similar reasons, the private ownership of land may have economic consequences for the government decisionmaker. Quite simply, Government may not be able to afford the process of land use decision making if its decisions are challenged by private owners who demand compensation for the effects of such decisions upon their rights 89/. The result thus may be that government involvement with land use regulation becomes economically impractical, with government financially unable to implement its land use policies and objectives. On the other hand, it can also be argued that Government should not be allowed to proceed in an unrestrained fashion vis-à-vis private property and thus should have to pay when its land use decisions result in a *de jure* or even a *de facto* taking of property.

88/ The issue of when - or if - government regulation of the use of land requires compensation to the owner, is an extraordinarily complex one. In Chapter VII of this work we shall explore the issue more thoroughly. For a complete treatment of the subject, we highly recommend, Keene, "Farmland Protection : Legal and Constitutional Issues", 15 Gonzaga Law Review 621 (1980); see also : Coughlin and Keene "The Protection of Farmland : A Reference Guidebook for State and Local Governments."

89/ Such a situation has in fact arisen in Samoa where government efforts to protect diminishing forests have stalled principally because any effort to establish forest reserve areas has been met with claims for compensation by persons or clans holding the *pule* (power) over land sought to be included within such reserves. Recent legislation drafted for the country attempts to deal with this problem by exempting government regulation (as distinguished from government taking) from the compensation provisions of the Taking of Land Act where such regulation does not entirely prohibit agriculture and related activities. See Section 55 of draft Samoa Water Resources Act, 1985.

In some countries, the result of these competing considerations is that a middle ground of accommodation has been reached with Government allowed (by legislation or the courts) to make land use decisions within specified limits that do not give rise to a right of compensation in private land owners 90/.

Finally, it is obvious that if extensive private landholdings are affected by Government land use decisions, there may be political consequences as well. Land is a fundamental commodity and decisions affecting its use are felt deeply by those who have an interest in it. Without detailing the variety of political consequences that could result, it is sufficient to note that strong feelings are rarely far below the surface when Government acts to exert control over land which people perceive as "theirs".

The foregoing is not to suggest, of course, that the political consequences of Government imposed changes in the use of privately held land will restrain the Government from acting. Indeed, considerable legislation attests to the fact that substantial changes may be worked in the way land is used, notwithstanding the fact that it is - or was - privately held. It may, for example, be expropriated and collectivized 91/. It may also be registered in the name of the Government and subsequently distributed for purposes the Government determines to be worthy 92/. It may be made the

---

90/ As we shall see, such a legal balance is being approached in those jurisdictions which have had to face the issue of land use decision making which impacts privately held land. There, the courts have held, in essence, that the exercise of government regulatory power over land does not give rise to a right of compensation when such exercise merely limits - but does not destroy - the economic value of the land. See also, fn 55 supra.

91/ See, e.g., Section 3 (1) of Ethiopia Proclamation 31 (1975) "Providing for the Public Ownership of Rural Lands". See also Articles 3 and 7 of Togo Ordonnance 78-18, "Portant Création et Mise en Valeur des Zones d'Aménagement Agricole Planifié".

92/ Section 4 of the Unregistered Land Act of Sudan (1970).

subject of consolidation and redistribution [93/]. It may be made the subject of a regulatory order which require specific protective measures or changes in farming procedure in order to protect the soil [94/]. And, it may be made the subject of a plan intended to achieve one or more of the development policies heretofore discussed [95/]. Thus, while private ownership may impose certain restraints on the land use decision-making process which would not exist if the land were government owned, even private ownership may not long-delay a government intent upon effecting changes in the way land is used.

2. Who Controls the Use of Land In Fact ?

A question which is related to the issue of who owns the land in the legal sense is who possesses or controls the land in fact. The question is posed for the purpose of illustrating that, in connection with land use, the tenure which exists in the legal sense is not necessarily what is found in practice.

93/ See Titles IV and VI of the Peruvian Land Reform Act (Act No. 17.716, 1969), Section 5 of the Cyprus Land Consolidation Law (No. 24 of 1969).

94/ See Section 16 of the Botswana Agricultural Resources Conservation Act (1974).

95/ The Land Development Act of Thailand, for example, authorizes:

> "planning for the utilization of land, the development of land and the specifying of areas for land utilization for submission to the Council of Ministers for approval in order that the state agency concerned may carry out." Section 5 (1).

See also Section 7 (f) of the proposed National Water Resources Law of Somalia and Chapters VI and VII of the proposed Waters Enactment of Malaysia which establish statutory authority for the preparation of water resources development plans that include detailed land use controls intended to protect watercourses and watersheds.

For example, it may be provided by statute that the owner of land is the government. In practice, however, the land may be used according to custom by others who develop an economic - or even emotional - attachment to it. A good example is found in the Sudan. There, under the terms of the Unregistered Lands Act, the Government is the legal owner of the vast majority of the country's rural, arable land 96/. In fact, however, the Government exerts actual control over a very much smaller proportion of farmable land. The remainder is in fact used by a multitude of private persons who either exert continuous control or who are nomadic and make only seasonal use. In either case, the use is likely to be in accordance with unwritten, customary practice 97/, and not under some statutory authorization.

96/ The Unregistered Lands Act (Act No. 23 of 1970) is the successor to the Land Settlement and Registration Act of 1925. The latter had provided for the registration of land in the name of particular individuals as well as the preservation and recording of servitudes and other rights, including customary rights. In practice, however, very little land and few rights were registered under the 1925 law; partly perhaps because the registration procedure was cumbersome, partly because communications were not good and partly perhaps because many of those the law was intended to benefit were illiterate and could not understand the provisions drafted for their protection. Whatever the reasons, the 1925 law did relatively little to provide certainty of tenure. The 1970 legislation then adopted a radical solution to the problem by declaring that all unregistered land (more than 90 percent of the Sudan, in fact) would henceforth be, "the property of the Government and shall be deemed to have been registered as such, as if the provisions of the Land Settlement and Registration Act have been duly complied with". Section 4.

97/ Customary practices in the Sudan range from the right of occupation and cultivation known as the right of *amara* to the use of newly formed lands in the Nile river (*Hag Elgusad*) to *Hag Elseluka*, the continued use of land theretofore cultivated, to the right to cultivate trees and take their produce - even if they are located on land registered in the name of another (*Hag Seluku*). Finally, *Hag Elharam* prohibits the demarcation by government officers of lands immediately surrounding a village (a *haram*) and thus prohibits the allotment of such lands to new investors.

Investigation may also reveal that land use among private persons is far different in practice that it is on paper. Nominally, ownership may be spread among relatively few people who are, in fact, absentee owners. In practice, the land may be occupied and farmed by numerous people who are tenants of the legal owner [98/]. Thus, a land use decision intended to bring about changes in farming practices by land owners may be misdirected if, in fact, lands are farmed by tenants. Similarly, a decision which affects the terms of ownership may produce an unintended economic and social impact upon tenants. Increasing the land taxes paid by owners, for instance, might raise revenues. It might also, however, result in rent increases and eventual impoverishment or displacement of tenants, thus creating a need for government support of such people. Finally, a land use decision intended to stimulate capital investment on farms may fail if the farms are occupied in fact by tenants who have no interest in the land they cultivate or are owned by absentees to whom capital investment is merely an impediment to a maximized rate of rent.

In short, it is not enough to identify legal ownership. Indeed, by itself, evidence of statutory ownership may yield a misleading impression of the actual state of agrarian production. It may also mask the need for tenurial reforms that are essential before certain land development policies can be carried forward.

98/ The abundance of "land to the tiller" legislation plainly suggests that the situation of asbtenteeism is a relatively frequent occurence. See, e.g. Sections 1 and 2 of Algerian Ordinance No. 71-73 on the Agrarian Revolution (1971); Article 1 of Peruvian Act No. 17.716 : The Land Reform Act (1969); Section 10 of Indonesian Act No. 5 Concerning Basic Regulations on Agrarian Principles (1960); and Ethopian Proclamation No. 31 of 1975 to Provide for the Public Ownership of Rural Lands.

3. How are customary rights integrated into the existing statutory law ?

A different set of restraints may be imposed upon the land use decision-making process by another type of tenure found in some developing countries. In Africa, particularly, there are many countries which have customary systems of land tenure. Among them are Cameroon, Ghana, Nigeria, Tanzania, Botswana, Zambia, Ivory Coast, Benin, Congo, Niger, Burkina Faso, the Central African Republic, Kenya, Uganda, Sudan and Lesotho [99/]. Nor is the amount of land under such tenure insignificant. In Zambia, for example, the area over which customary land law has operated, is approximatly 94 percent of the total country [100/]. In Cameroon, it has been as high as 99 percent [101/]. Thus, it is imperative to evaluate the customary tenure system as well as the customary land laws which provide the framework for the system's operation.

While the specifics of customary tenure will of course vary from case to case, there are certain distinct features which generally tend to distinguish customary tenure from western systems of tenure. *Inter alia*, the customary system is founded upon the principle of the "community interest" rather than an advantage to a particular individual. The determination of where the community interest lies, moreover, is frequently a prerogative of the traditional chief who, in reaching such a determination, applies applicable customary law. That law, while well understood by members of the social group, is usually unwritten.

Because it is unwritten and sometimes informally applied (at least by western-influenced standards) customary law - and thus the framework of the customary system - could be forgotten or ignored when land use decisions are reached. It is this possibility of slighting the customary system that could produce a confrontational result when governmental land use decisions and

---

99/ See Mifsud, "Customary Land Law in Africa", FAO, 1967, p. 9.

100/ *Ibid*, p. 8.

101/ *Ibid*., pp. 5, 6.

customary land tenure systems intersect. For the fact is that despite its unwritten, informal and sometimes vague character, the customary land tenure system has provided one of the principal institutional frameworks for the rapid social changes that have occurred throughout Africa in the second half of this century [102/]. The customary system has tended to suppress the phenomenon of absentee landlordism and land speculation and has prevented land grabbing on a large scale. It has also tended to consolidate the adhesion of the social group which - in recent times especially - has been threatened by a variety of natural and man-made forces. Thus, simply imposing a more formalized process of land use decisions-making through new legislation, without giving regard to existing systems of tenure and their customary law underpinnings, could well result in the destruction of one of the main supports of social stability in the rural sector.

One way some developing countries have sought to minimize the risk of destroying of the customary tenure system is to formalize the system through legislation. In Botswana, for example, Parliament has passed the Tribal Land Act (Cap. 32:02 of 1970) which establishes tribal land boards and gives them the powers vested in a tribal chief under customary law with regard to the granting, variation and determination of customary forms of tenure of land [103/]. Those powers include granting rights to the use of tribal land, cancelling rights to use such land and the resolution of appeals from decisions by any lesser authority concerning the granting or cancellation of rights to use tribal land [104/]. In addition, the Act requires each land board to determine the boundaries of the grazing lands within the tribal areas under its jurisdiction and insulates such areas from encroachment by limiting the granting of rights of use for horticultural purposes [105/]. Insofar as the granting of rights of use is concerned, the land boards are also empowered

---

102/ See Mifsud, "Customary Land Law in Africa", FAO, 1967, p. 2.

103/ Tribal Land Act, Secs. 3, 12 and 13.

104/ *Ibid.*, Sec. 13.

105/ *Ibid.*, Sec. 17.

to issue short-term leases of small parcels (not exceeding 5 acres in size) and may issue longer term leases only subject to approval by higher authority 106/. Further, the law makes it clear that it is tribesmen who are the intended beneficiaries by providing that no land may be granted or leased except to a tribesman without the express prior consent of the Minister 107/. Finally, the Act provides for the granting of tribal land to the State where the public interest so requires, but confirms that where such land is subject to customary rights of tenure, the occupier of such land shall be granted a right of use to other land of equivalent value 108/. Moreover, any such person must be compensated for the value of any standing crops or improvements made to the land taken over by the State 109/.

Legislation of the type exemplified by the Botswana law thus seeks to avoid a confrontation between holders of land under customary tenure and the land use development process by : 1) giving customary rights a statutory basis as substantial as that enjoyed by the proponents of non-tribal development; 2) giving tribesmen a preference in the leasing and granting of tribal lands; and 3) providing compensation in money or in kind to those whose customary rights are taken by the State.

With the Botswana example in mind, we believe it is useful to investigate the extent to which the existing legal system provides the opportunity to "legitimize" customary rights. Does the existing system, for example, provide an adjudication procedure which enables an applicant in possession of a customary right to confirm or "quiet" his right against other claimants, actual or potential ? 110/. Does it provide for the registration

---

106/ Tribal Land Act, Secs. 3, 12 and 13, Secs. 23 and 24.

107/ *Ibid*., Sec. 31.

108/ Botswana Tribal Land Act, Sec. 33.

109/ *Ibid*.

110/ See, for instance, the Kenya Lands Adjudication Ordinance, 1959; the Uganda Crown Lands Rules, 1958 and Sections 15 and 19 of the Sudan Land Settlement and Registration Ordinance, 1925, which provided for a quasi-judicial settlement process involving a "settlement officer" who established the existence of a customary right in accordance with procedures applicable to the hearing of civil suits. Such establishment in fact, involved the setting aside of certain land as "haram" (see fn. 97 *supra*.).

(or <u>immatriculation</u> in the French legislation) of title ? 111/. Generally speaking, registration follows an adjudication that a person may be recognized as the owner of land by native custom 112/, and is thus, in effect, the conclusion, of the process of adjudication.

Legislative efforts to avoid destruction of an existing system of customary tenure may take other forms as well. Rather than adjudicating rights, the law may make provision for the grant of a title to land which is expressly based upon the fact of actual possession 113/. This <u>de jure</u> recognition of <u>de facto</u> possession differs from registration in that registration accords few, if any, presumptive rights to the occupier who still must "prove" his right in an adjudicating proceeding.

A related form of legislation is that known colloquially as "Land to the Tiller". Essentially this type of legislation arises out of landlord-tenant relationships which are distinguished by the tenant's obligation to perform agricultural work on the landlord's fields. As Mifsud notes, such relationships were sometimes connected with a political

---

111/ In the case of registration, the purpose is not simply to register - which is an essentially administrative act - but rather, to provide security to the holder of title and to facilitate dealings in the land. The effect, in sum, is far reaching and takes the land out of the sphere of customary law altogether, insofar as tenure is concerned. See Mifsud, "Customary Land Law in Africa", p. 31.

112/ See, e.g., Sections 11 and 17 of the Crown Lands Rules, 1958; Section 11, Native Reserves and Native Trust Land (Adjudication and Titles) Ordinance of Zambia.

113/ Loi No. 59-131, 10.10 (1959) of Tunisia, for example, provides that every cultivator peacefully occupying land in good faith for a period of 5 years prior to enactment of the law - but without title of ownership - could obtain a "Certificate of Possession". The Certificate is personal to the holder and may not be transferred. It does, however, enable the holder to obtain credit by pledging the property as security. See Mifsud, "Customary Land Law in Africa", p.35.

organization of society based on a hierarchy of chiefs and the existence of a caste which was socially and economically ascendant 114/. Land to the Tiller laws thus do tend to respect customary practices in the sense that they grant title to those occupying land as a result of the customary system. On the other hand, they obviously are contrary to such practices in the sense that they transfer title from those who held it under the customary system to those who did not. The important consideration here, though, is that such laws frequently derive from a customary system.

This work is not intended as an exhaustive treatise on the subject of customary land laws. Others have dealt with the subject and should be consulted for a detailed comparison and analysis of customary practices *inter se*. The point to be made here, however - and one that we hope this brief discussion has served to emphasize - is that customary practice is an important issue to consider when evaluating the land use decision making process. Depending upon the country or region, it may be factor at least as significant as existing land development legislation. Indeed, where distances are great, infrastructure is poor and enforcement weak, customary practice may be of much greater significance than laws found in a seldom consulted code book in the capital city.

114/ Customary Land Law in Africa, p. 38.

CHAPTER V - LAND USE PLANS : WHAT DO THEY DO AND HOW ARE THEY MADE ?

In this chapter, we shift our focus a little. Heretofore, we have stressed the importance of acquiring an understanding of 1) government policies and priorities concerning land; 2) existing land use decision-making mechanisms; and 3) existing land tenure patterns and customary practices. Investigation of these basic subjects is necessary, we believe to provide the factual foundation which must exist befor work can begin on improvements to the procedure and substance of the land use decision-making process. Once a review of the existing land use situation has occurred, the legislative drafter should be ready to begin the job of creating a decision-making structure which alters the status quo to produce more rational determinations of how to use land. It is to that subject which we now turn, beginning with an analysis of the land use plan.

Almost inevitably, the effort to rationalize land use decision-making will become involved with the development of land use plans. Because the technical officials of many developing countries are familiar with 3 or 5 or 10 year economic development (and other) plans, counterpart personnel will have an awareness of - if not a predilection for - the concept of master planning. Moreover, a land use plan can serve as the engine which reforms and revitalizes and thus improves the process of land use decision-making process. Until recently, however, learning about land use plans was a bit like trying to understand the facts of life for the first time - a lot of people talked about it, but almost nobody told you how to do it. Fortunately, this situation has been largely rectified. In the last four years, at least three major efforts have been made to provide instruction in "how to do it". One of these, entitled Guidelines for Land Use Planning, is a 1985 FAO publication that concisely takes the reader through a step-by-step discussion of the preparation of a plan. The second work entitled An Introduction to Development Planning in the Third World [115/] is a study of the philosophy and methodology of land use planning in developing countries. While not a

---

115/ By Diana Conyers and Peter Hills, John Wiley and Sons, 1984.

step-by-step approach like the FAO work, it nonetheless makes a readable presentation of the techniques of data collection and analysis which are normally used by experienced planners in preparing a land use plan. Finally, the work On Rational Grounds (Systems Analysis in Catchment Land Use Planning) 116/ presents a more technical discussion of the development of a land use plan in practice. Less a theoretical work than the other two publications, it discusses land use planning in the context of an actual plan of development in Western Australia.

Apart from the general background knowledge which the above works can provide, we believe it also important for the person drafting land use legislation to have more specific knowledge of several factors involved in the construction of a land use plan. Such knowledge is important, we believe, because it pertains to matters which are likely to be dealt with directly by statute. While these matters are covered to some degree by the above-cited works, they tend to submerge issues which have relevance to the lawyer since they are not drafted from the legal perspective. Because a clear understanding of these subjects is important to the subject of legal drafting, we have elected to present them in some detail in the pages which follow.

1. Scale of the Plan

Our discussions with planners and other technical people involved in the rural land development process have continually served to emphasize one critical point about land use plans : there are many kinds of plans and the

---

116/ By David Bennett and Jonh F. Thomas, of the CSIRO Division of Land Resources Management, Perth Western Australia, published by Elsevier Scientific Publishing Company, 1982.

purpose of any particular plan is largely determined by its scale. Thus, for example, there are regional land use development plans (sometimes called "global plans") whose purpose is usually identification : what areas are suitable for certain crops and what areas need to be protected from overgrazing or shifting cultivation. Typically such plans are prepared at a scale of 1,000,000:1 and can be developed through use of remote sensing technology (frequently LANDSAT photographs are used) with some on-the-ground verification of satellite imaging.

In the medium range are "site identification" plans developed at a scale of 50,000:1, which are typically specific to an area and specific to a form of development. Thus, such medium range plans could be used to determine what parcels of land within a larger area should be drained to permit economical cultivation or what lands are suitable for development as cattle range. Normally such medium scale plans make greater use of on-the-ground surveys than remote sensing materials, although the latter may be helpful to narrow the spectrum of land under consideration.

Third, at the smallest end of the scale are the "detailed plans" which are typically developed at a scale of 10,000:1. Such plans are usually considered to be operational plans and will indicate where construction is to take place, where ploughing should occur, where pipes should be laid and fences erected, and so forth. Such plans are normally developed by on-the-ground survey work exclusively.

The second truism of importance for the lawyer or planner on the subject of scale is that time and expense are usually inversely proportional to the scale of the plan under consideration. Thus, for example, it will take relatively longer and be more expensive to produce a medium range "site identification" plan than a global (regional) land use plan. In part this is because of the nature of the work involved : the larger scale relies more heavily upon extant data produced by machinery whose capital costs have been fronted by someone else, whereas the smaller scale plan is much more labor intensive and frequently is based upon data which must be generated for the first time as part of the planning process.

An additional reality which must be confronted is that plans of different scale are usually not interchangeable. Thus, for example, neither a global plan nor a site identification plan will provide the kind of detail necessary for on-the-ground implementation of a project. Similarly, an operational plan would be of little use in identifying areas to be protected from overgrazing or suitable for certain crops. A medium-scale site identification plan might contribute to such a large scale evaluation but, practically, speaking, the cost in terms of both money and time to piece together a global plan from several smaller-scale site plans would be prohibitive.

The lack of interchangeability among plans leads to the final truism relevant to the subject of scale : the utility of the planning process will be increased if plans of different scale are linked to provide a continuum from the regional (or national) determination of objectives, through the identification of suitable sites to carry out such objectives, to the detailed planning of projects necessary for actual implementation. Thus, the development of land use plans, itself begins to resemble a process which can be represented thusly:

SCALE

Regional/Global (Phase I)

↓

Site Specific/Project I.D. Planning (Phase II)

↓

Detailed (Operational) Planning (Phase III)

Unfortunately, this picture is oversimplified since it fails to include one kink which has worked itself into the development of medium range (site specific) plans. Once regional planning has occured and areas suitable for different kinds of development (or protection) have been selected, planners have frequently found themselves facing a choice regarding the preparation medium scale plans : should those plans focus on a particular geographic area or should they instead focus on a particular sector of development such as irrigation or range or rainfed agriculture.

From a systems approach, it probably makes more sense to plan on an area-wide basis. Developments, after all, do not exist in isolation; rather, they interact. The development of rainfed agriculture, for instance, may adversely impact grazing and, at the same time, create a need for improved infrastructure to move the crop to market. The development of irrigation facilities would probably generate the same - or similar - issues. A medium scale plan utilizing an "area" approach would be more likely to use a systems approach and thus examine these related factors. So why then do planners hesitate before choosing such an approach to medium scale planning ?. The answer appears to be that financing agencies - particularly the banks - prefer sectoral rather than area development. Thus, they are more likely to finance the planning (and development) of the irrigation or rainfed <u>sectors</u> rather than integrated development in a particular sub-regional area. Why this is so is unclear. For the lawyer and the planner, however, it is a fact of life which must be taken into account when considering the development of land use plans. When it is considered thusly, the tension between medium range <u>areal</u> planning on the one hand and medium range <u>sectoral</u> planning on the other, results in a diagram of the plan process that looks something like the following :

SCALE

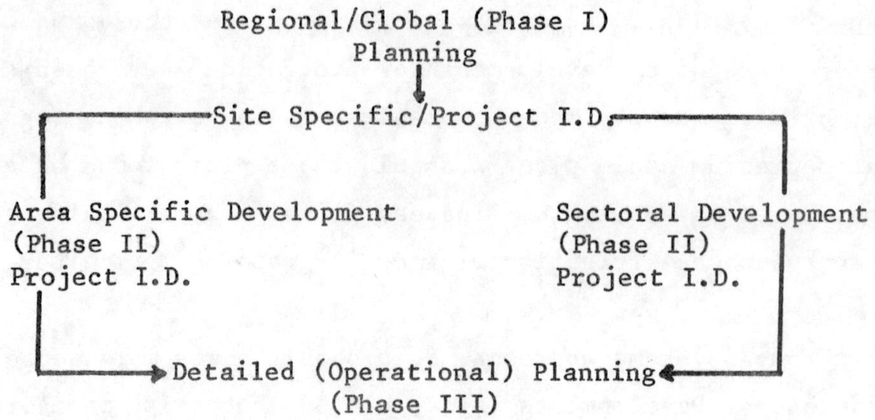

So what do all of these various truisms and choices related to scale mean to the drafting or implementation of legislation ? First, they suggest that legislation should be clear in its purpose regarding the preparation of a land use plan. If the intent of the legislation is simply to guide the government in making choices generally about what lands to develop, what lands to protect and which crops to promote, a global plan may be enough. If, on the other hand the intention is to draft legislation which will authorize and direct the preparation of a plan that shows specifically what acreage should be developed and with what specific kinds of development projects (irrigated agriculture, rainfed, maize, cotton, etc.) then a global plan will probably not be enough. Instead a more detailed site-specific plan will be required, and the legislation should so provide.

Second, the factors discussed above make it apparent that different types of plans cannot be lumped together under the same methodology and provided with the same time frame for completion. Site specific plans take longer and are produced in a far different way than global plans. Operational plans, in turn, are drastically different from medium scale plans. Moreover, the different focus of each type of plan suggests that each may logically be prepared at a different level. Global/national plans, if national in both scope and objective, would appear to be suitable for preparation at the national level. Global/regional plans or site specific plans, on the other hand, could be more profitably prepared at the sub-national level or with considerable sub-national input, if the national government insists on keeping its hand in.

The fact that plans tend not to be interchangeable - yet may be linked - also has legislative significance. If more than global planning is anticipated, then a legislative provision expressly providing for the linkage of plans, is worth considering. While it might be argued that such detail is beyond the ambit of a land use planning law, the fact is that a variety of national planning legislation already specifies, in some detail, the steps to be taken in producing required plans [117/]. Further, the existence of a choice of approaches to medium scale planning (area specific, versus sectoral) reveals another use for proposed legislation. If, in fact, area specific planning is a more rational approach to choosing development projects than sectoral planning, then there is no reason why such an approach should not be included in appropriate legislation. Indeed, one result of the statutory incorporation of such a systems-based approach might be to give governments additional leverage in resisting outside forces seeking to compel adoption of a less useful approach to medium-scale planning.

In short, the concept of scale carries with it a variety of issues and concerns that are relevant to the land development process. Accordingly, we recommend that the scale of needed plans be given consideration when legislation is proposed.

2. Data Inputs Essential to a Rural Land Use Plan

Apart from considering the matter of scale, it also is useful to view land use plans as vehicles for answering certain questions relevant to development. In the remaining portion of this chapter we suggest, and briefly discuss, two of the questions with which a land use plan should be expected to grapple. These are : 1) What land resources do you have ? and 2) If the land is suitable for something, what is it ?

117/ See, for example, the Botswana Town and Country Planning Order (Statutory Instrument No. 97 of 1980); the Malaysia Town and Country Planning Act (Act No. 172 of 1976); draft Water Resources Act of Tonga (1985); and draft Water Resources Act of Samoa (1985).

The first of the above questions raises the obvious point that one cannot adequately plan the disposition of resources without knowing precisely what resources there are. In the case of land use plans, knowing what resources there are usually means obtaining data inputs of several distinct types. While the number and character of these inputs may vary according to the precise conditions of the area or region to be planned, most plans would appear to be deficient unless they included at least the following elements :

a) A cadastral survey. For the reasons discussed above in Chapter IV, it is extremely important to have a solid understanding of the nature of existing landholdings, their boundaries, and the political boundaries of the district or area to be planned. A cadastral survey is intended to produce such information.

b) Thematic maps. Thematic maps are intended to depict existing uses. A cropping map, for instance, will tend to show what crops are being grown, and where. An erosion map, on the other hand, will depict areas in which soil conservation is a problem. The relatively wide availability of LANDSAT data has greatly facilitated - at least on the global planning scale - the production of the maps needed to formulate national policy alternatives about where to grow certain crops and which lands (or regions) should receive priority attention regarding soil conservation. Smaller scale thematic maps intended for site specific planning, on the other hand, will likely require much more intensive ground survey work and thus, be slower and more expensive to produce.

c) Climatic data. Unless ample irrigation water is available, the frequency, quantity and pattern of rainfall is a fundamental input to any effort to plan the use of rural land. Similarly, if higher elevations are involved in the planning effort, the frequency and severity of freezing temperatures may be an important consideration. Thus, climatic data are an important element that should be included as an input to most land use plans.

d) Soils survey data. Soils are far from uniform in their characteristics. Indeed, within a relatively small area there may be considerable variation in porosity, compaction, water table level and salinity, among other things. In each case, these variations will influence the suitability of particular land for certain crops. One means of identifying these variations is through a system of taxonomic classification which lists soils as to type, e.g., clay or sand or gravel. As the taxonomic classification becomes more sophisiticated (in essence, as the scale of the classification diminishes) the evaluation of land quality becomes more precise. As a result, the ability to measure land suitability - the next major step in the planning process - will also increase. As is the case with planning scale, however, land classification becomes slower and more expensive when the desired level of detail increases.

e) A hydrologic survey. Finally, it is important to have some understanding of the availability of water resources to the region or areas for which a plan will be developed. In this context, "availability" means not only the physical presence of water in or near the area to be planned, but also the suitability of such water for the possible uses to which the land in issue may be part. Thus, the data input to the plan should include a hydrologic survey which covers not only the physical availability of water supplies; but also their quality. Further, if pertinent water supplies are subject to claims of prior use, whether based upon custom or statute, the supplies may not be "available" in the legal sense. Accordingly, where prior use may be an issue, the data input on water resources should include information on the relative amounts of physically available water supplies which are covered by prior rights, on the one hand, and which are surplus, on the other.

3. The Determination of Land Suitability

The above data inputs to a plan make it possible to determine the characteristics of the land and related resources which the plan is intended to affect. From that determination, it is possible to move on to the following question : if the land in issue is suitable for some kind of rural development, what is it ? In essence, the answer to the question depends upon a matching of 1) land characteristics with 2) land use requirements. Indeed, it is just such a matching exercise that planners undertake when they attempt to determine the suitability of land for certain uses. We illustrate.

Suppose the government decides to pursue a dual crop policy of growing maize for domestic consumption and irrigated cotton to generate export revenue. By so deciding, the government has made an initial choice about land use : it will pursue crop cultivation (i.e., agriculture) rather than meat production(grazing) or timber export (forestry). In addition, it has made a choice about land use types : from the realm of agricultural land use possibilities, it has decided to pursue the development of just two crops.

The science of agronomy tells us that the two desired crops will achieve optimum growth under certain conditions. From these conditions, it is possible to deduce their land use requirements. Thus, agronomists would tell us that maize is a highly salt sensitive crop with a relatively high demand for water in the early period of its growth cycle and a relatively low demand later. Cotton, on the other hand is a relatively more salt tolerant crop, but is also a crop which needs a more consistent supply of water throughout its growth cycle. From these characteristics, it is possible to conclude that maize has a land use requirement for soil which is relatively salt free in the root zone. Further, it is more likely to achieve optimum growth in an area where rain falls (or salt free irrigation water is available) in the early part of the growing season. Cotton, on the other hand can be grown in soil which may have a higher salt content (or irrigated with water which may be relatively more salty) but the land on which it is grown must have access to water throughout the growing season [118/].

In sum and substance, the determination of desireable land use characteristics has proceeded as follows :

<u>Land Use</u> (Agriculture)

↓

<u>Land Use Types</u>

Maize | Cotton

↓

<u>Land Use Requirements</u>

Maize	Cotton
1. Low soil salt content	1. Higher soil salt content acceptable
2. Abundant low salt water early in growth cycle	2. Abundant water available throughout growth cycle.

At the same time, provision of the data inputs described in the previous section permits a parallel determination of land characteristics. Thus, from a basic determination that the government would focus upon the development of land, global planning would enable planners to make a further determination of which lands should be the subject of the plan. Thereafter, the data inputs previously described permit a description of <u>characteristics</u> for the lands being studied. Thus, for instance, particular lands may be classed according to the amount of rainfall received and its timing, the availability and quality of surface and underground water supplies or the mineral content of the soil.

118/ For the purposes of this example, we have simplified the land use characteristics applicable to the two crops. In reality, each crop may have many more land use characteristics associated with it.

This parallel determination of land characteristics can be depicted in the following way :

Land
↓
Land Units to be planned
↓
Land Characteristics
(1) soil salinity
(2) rainfall
(3) available surface and groundwater
(4) compaction/porosity.

The planner in our example would thus be in possession of two groupings of data : 1) data which depicts the land use requirements for growing maize on the one hand and cotton on the other, and 2) data which sets forth the land characteristics for various potential growing sites. Schematically, the processes used to obtain these two groupings of data can be arranged as follows :

LAND USE (Agriculture) → LAND USE TYPES

Maize, Cotton → Land Use Requirements

Maize	Cotton
1. Low soil salt	2. Higher soil salt
2. Abundant early water	2. Abundant water throughout growth cycle

LAND → LAND UNITS TO BE PLANNED → Land Characteristics

1. Soil Salinity
2. Rainfall
3. Available Surface and Groundwater
4. Compaction/Porosity.

Land Use Requirements → Land Suitability ← Land Characteristics

As the schematic demonstrates, land suitability is the end result of the two parallel efforts to develop data about land use requirements and land characteristics. It is, in sum, a process of making cross comparisons between land use requirements and land characteristics in order to get a proper fit. From such a comparison it is possible to reach the conclusion that, for example, a particular area of land is suitable for growing a certain range of specific crops or, in the alternative, that a specific crop is suitable for growing on a variety of specific lands. From either perspective, the determination of suitability is likely to result in a range of alternatives: alternative use choices for a particular land site, or alternative land sites for a particular use.

Exactly how the land development process should now select between and among competing alternative uses or sites is the subject of the following chapter. Before we turn to that subject, however, we believe it is worthwhile to briefly explore how the data inputs and land suitability evaluations discussed above are relevant to the drafting of legislation.

One of the important functions of planning legislation is to guide the individuals who are involved in making decisions about land. Planning can be a confusing business in the best of times and, with political and social concerns thrown into the mix, it becomes even easier to lose one's way. It would seem obvious that competent land use planning could not take place in the absence of the several data inputs described in the second part of this chapter. Under the pressure to make a decision about land now, however, there may be a very strong tendency to short cut essential data inputs - or even to eliminate them altogether.

In these circumstances, writing minimum data input requirements into the law will do several things. First, it will provide guidance to the country's planners who may not be familiar with the land use planning process. More importantly, it will create a legal obligation to include such inputs whatever plans are produced. The existence of such an obligation means several things. First, it means that technical officials will be on solid legal ground if they resist political and social pressures to build a quick and dirty data base in order to produce quick - or preordained - results. Providing such inputs, inotherwords is not an option to be pursued only when circumstances permit. It is an unwaivable requirement to be pursued notwithstanding the fact that an important minister wants a plan, *post haste*. Further, the existence of a legal obligation to construct a competent data base for decision-making purposes may increase the leverage technical personnel can exert in seeking to obtain training or expert assistance if existing local talent is not sufficient to acquire or evaluate necessary data inputs. Such leverage may be greatly increased, too, if the legislation provides that development may not proceed except in accordance with the provisions of a land use plan which is based upon the data inputs described in the law. In effect then, the building of an adequate data base is made a prerequisite for development.

Making legislative provision for an express determination of land suitability also serves several purposes. As is the case with requiring certain data inputs, prescribing the necessity of making a determination of suitability serves the purpose of educating less than expert officials in how a land use plan is put together. Moreover, it tends to encourage the development of land use *alternatives* and thus works against efforts to use the planning process as a kind of *post hoc* rationalization of a pre-determined choice. Finally, requiring a determination of suitability opens a door for considering other factors of importance to making rational choices about land. For example, "suitability" may be defined in the legislation to include social and environmental compatibility. In this way, the law can broaden the scope of a process that would otherwise be limited to a determination of technical feasability.

CHAPTER VI - MAKING THE CHOICE : SELECTING FROM AMONG COMPETING LAND USE ALTERNATIVES

In our work we occasionally observe a phenomenon which sometimes overtakes land use planning projects in developing countries. After the data inputs have occurred and land suitability evaluations have been made, progress stops. When the government begins to press for a plan which proposes specific land uses, nothing emerges. Instead, another round of data collection begins in an effort to "refine" the inputs already made. As government pressure for decisions mounts, the renewed data collection effort becomes more and more feverish. Finally, when the last of the project's dollars have been spent, there is a veritable mountain of data, terrifically refined determinations about land suitability - and still no recommendations about what land uses ought to be occuring on which lands. The planning effort, in short, has been unable to move beyond the data collection and evaluation stage.

No doubt, the reasons for this failure may be linked in-part to the particular personalities involved in the planning effort. It is our suspicion, however, that there is often a more fundamental problem which leads to this decision-making paralysis.

Data collection and evaluation is a relatively neutral, non-controversial operation. On the whole, it smacks of applied science and is not especially likely to get those who engage in it into much difficulty. Actually making choices between and among alternatives produced from matching up land characteristics and land use requirements, however, is a different matter. Choosing one alternative means rejecting another and that other may have its proponents. Moving beyond an evaluation of land suitability thus entails certain risks not present during earlier steps in the decision-making process.

Moreover, it also appears to be the case that relatively less guidance is available on the subject of choosing from among alternative land uses. Since the end of the Second World War, great strides have been made in the techniques of data collection and computer assisted data analysis. With time and testing, these advances have gained fairly wide acceptance and have been taught to subsequent generations of technical personnel. The result is that technical people are comfortable with these new techniques and thus tend to use them.

By way of contrast, there appears to be much uncertainty about how to actually make choices once alternative land uses have been produced through application of the aforementioned technical advances. Perhaps because making choices often involves non-technical matters that do not easily lend themselves to technological advances, progress in this part of the land development process has not kept pace with that recorded in connection with the precursors to decision-making. The result is that planners sometimes finish their data collecting and evaluating work and find themselves facing uncertain terrain without much guidance when it comes to making choices from among the alternatives their work has produced.

The problem which blunts further progress in some land use planning projects is thus two-fold. It is on the one hand a problem of the political risk inherent in selecting from among alternatives. It is, on the other hand, a problem of a lack of procedural and substantive guidance in actually making the choice. When these two elements combine, some technical personnel tend to view the process of making choices about land with considerable trepidation and thus may postpone the day of judgement as long as possible.

Perhaps not surprisingly, it is our view that appropriately drafted legislation can assist in resolving both parts of the above problem and thus get the land use planning effort moving if it has come to halt or; even better, keep it from coming to stop in the first place. This assistance, we believe, should be directed at two goals : 1) building a consensus about the use of land, thus incidentally reducing the risk to the decision-maker and 2) providing procedural and substantive principles which serve to guide the process of choosing between alternative land uses.

1. The Building of a Consensus about How to Use Land

The issue of building a consensus about recommended land uses - particularly those which require changes in the way land is currently used - goes beyond reduction of the political risk to the decision-maker. As noted in the overview chapter which began this work, development of a consensus about land use decisions is highly important where infrastructure is poor, enforcement mechanisms are weak and hostility to government policy may limit its impact to the four walls of the government ministry from whence it was developed. In such a situation - which is often the status quo in many developing countries - building a consensus about the use of land is much more than a procedural nicety; it is a basic prerequisite to a self-enforcing programme of land use planning.

So how then is a consensus built and what is the relevancy of legislation to the effort ?

In our view, building a consensus about the use of land means involving those individuals who are likely to be affected by government decisions about the use of land. It means a sharing of the decision-making power between professional planners or other technical personnel on the one hand and, on the other, those who are expected to abide by the decisions which are made i.e., the rural inhabitants whose farming, grazing, forestry and other agrarian activities may be impacted. Suggesting the inclusion of rural people in the decision-making process, however, leaves open a number of questions including, where, when and how such people should be brought into the process.

From our discussion of the concept of scale, it will be recalled that there are likely to be several "levels" of plans ranging from global or national plans at the larger end of the scale, to site specific project identification plans at the middle range, to project implementation plans - akin to building plans - at the smallest scale. No doubt there may be some value in bringing rural residents to the global planning process; they may, for instance, contribute an understanding of certain customary practices which could have bearing on government land policies - even at the national level. In general, however, we believe that rural dwellers are not especially likely to be interested in the development of national agricultural policies. Moreover, it may be difficult to bring rural dwellers regularly to the place where global plans are being prepared (possibly a capital city located many kilometers from the rural dweller's village). Thus, it is probable that the marginal cost of rural participation in the development of global plans may exceed the marginal benefit of such participation.

What rural dwellers are most likely to be interested in is the plan for the development of their land - which may be "theirs" by either statute or custom. Thus, rural dwellers will without doubt have an interest in - and be extremely important to the implementation of - medium range plans that actually identify the site of proposed agrarian activities [119/]. Similarly, the government's interest in having public involvement is likely to be substantial at the medium range level since it is here, at the project siting stage, that local people can most readily frustrate the planning effort by, for example, ignoring government efforts to, promote a particular crop or maintain certain lands for grazing or demarcate other lands for rainfed agriculture. In sum, it is at the project site identification stage that rural people should most want to participate and that government should most desire their participation.

119/ This interest may also extend to the development of project implementation plans. In this regard we have purposely emphasized the word "may". Some interest is likely to occur in such detailed plans simply because they relate to activities on local land. Similarly, because government sponsored employment may result there may be added interest. Finally, to the extent that permanent construction (of structures, irrigation laterals, etc.) may ensure, there is likely to be a local interest in having it sited correctly. On he other hand, local citizens may not have much interest int he engineering or architectural work involved. Nor may they are much about the bidding process for contractors and equipment supplies. Thus, the interest is likely to be more particularized.

Exactly when and how rural people should be brought into medium range planning is not subject to an answer that will apply to all situations. Clearly, of course, public involvement should occur before final decisions are made. If it is intended that the public simply rubber-stamp planning decisions already reached by the government, it is unlikely that much of a consensus will be built. More probably, local people will perceive how they are being used and will respond with resentment and opposition.

On the other hand, it is also probable that local people - as a group - will lack the discipline (and the time) to put together themselves a first draft medium range plan that conforms to a global plan developed at the national level. More fruitfully, a first draft should be constructed with technical personnel, but with several caveats. First, the draft should be constructed at the level of government which 1) contains competent planning personnel; and 2) is closest to the land. Our rationale for emphasizing proximity to the land is that the closer officials are physically the more likely they are to understand local problems, local customs, local needs and the local psyche. In our view, the more such factors are taken into account, the more likely it is that a locally acceptable (and thus self-enforcing) land use plan will be developed. Thus if there is a regional, provincial or state level of government, and that level includes competent technical personnel (something which the lawyer is unlikely to learn except by talking and evaluating the people at that level) then it should be <u>that</u> level - not the national government - which is assigned responsibility for preparing the first draft medium range plan. If there is a level of government even closer to the land e.g. a district or local council, and that level is found to contain competent technical planning personnel, then it should be <u>that</u> level, rather than the higher regional, provincial or state government which is given responsibility for producing the medium range plan.

Second, if a level of government other than the lowest level (i.e., the level closest to the land) is provided with medium range planning responsibility, it should include representatives from any lower level as part of the group which actually constructs the first draft site selection plan. The fact is that perspectives change at different levels of government. Building a consensus in part means understanding - and where possible, following - the point of view of those who work the land. That point of view is more likely to be expressed by those closest to the farmer. Thus, one way of hearing that view is to include those most likely to express it. One means of doing this is to include in the planning group lower level technical personnel who work regularly with agriculturalists. Another way of course is to include a representative of the farmers themselves. If there are farmers associations or agricultural cooperative groups, it may be appropriate to include one or more of their members in the group which produces a first draft plan. If there are no such groups, it may be appropriate to provide for their organization in order that farmers, pastoralists and other agriculturalists may participate and be heard.

Finally, while the draft plan should be produced in accordance with a number of basic principles - which we discuss below - it is essential to remember that the plan should benefit local people. Unfortunately this rather obvious principle often gets lost in the struggle to plan for an enfranchised peasantry, a stronger agricultural sector or a self-reliant nation. The simple fact is, though, that unless the plan benefits local people - and equally important, that local people can <u>perceive</u> the benefit of the plan to themselves - they will not support it. Worse, they may resist it. Thus, whatever, its laudable national or regional purpose, the medium range plan, to succeed, must embrace the basic principle that it will benefit those lands or rights to use land which are affected. If it fails in this, it is unlikely to succeed in other respects.

Heretofore we have described the land use plan under consideration as a "draft" plan. The term is used to distinguish a plan prepared by government planners or other technicians (whether or not assisted by representatives of local people) from a plan which has been considered, criticized and discussed by local people themselves in a forum created for that purpose. In our view a "draft plan" does not mature into a "plan" until its creators have put it into the public crucible; that is, until local people, have had the opportunity to weigh-in with their comments, and until the plan's creators have had to consider those comments and evaluate possible changes based thereon.

We want to be clear on this point because the message being conveyed is not necessarily a popular one with government officials and the lawyer or planner who presents it will almost certainly be put on the defensive. Nonetheless it is our experience that a consensus about land use decisions is much more likely to develop if local people - particularly those whose lands or rights to use land are in issue - are approached and listened to before the proposed decisions of the plan are cast in concrete. Perhaps for this reason, more modern land use legislation requires that a proposed plan be presented to the public in draft and that interested members of the public or their representatives - either in writing or at hearing conducted for the purpose - be given the opportunity to voice their objections 120/.

120/ See, for example, Section 54 of proposed National Water Resources Legislation for Samoa (FAO 1984) which requires government planning officials seeking to establish a watershed protection zone to seek the views of any owner of land (including village customary lands) included within the proposed zone. Following that discussion, the proponent of the plan is required to conduct a hearing and to consider any such views expressed. *Id.* Based upon that consideration, the proposed zone may be rejected or modified to take the said views into account. *Id.* See also Section 9, the Town and Country Planning Act of Malaysia which requires notice and an opportunity to be heard regarding the promulgation of structure plans for development in the rural sector; the Nepal Decentralization Act (1982) Section 14, which provides for formulation of village development plans by locally elected panchayats; the Cyprus Land Consolidation Land (1969) which provides for the participation of landowners in the consolidation of land through mutual agreement (Section 3); and the Land Reform Act of Peru (1969) which gives landowners the opportunity to raise various technical and social objections to government plans for land reform.

Thus, for the lawyer or planner the challenge is to design and implement a law which opens up a decision-making process that is in fact easier to run when it excludes the public. Ideally the decision-making process will thus include statutory procedures which compel government officials to submit their plans to public scrutiny and to listen to public objections before the plan is adopted. It is not a procedure that officials will find especially comfortable; listening to criticism rarely is. It will be, however, a process much more likely to produce the two-way flow of information from which a consensus can be developed.

One note of caution should finally be expressed before we move on to the subject of planning principles to be incorporated in legislation. It must be kept in mind that the point of public involvement is to produce a better plan that will be supported by local land users when the time comes for implementation. Public participation, inotherwords, is goal oriented. Accordingly,the lawyer or planner should also be prepared to draft reasonable limitations which maintain public participation as a means to an end and thus prevent it from becoming the end itself. Inotherwords, while a public hearing is probably appropriate for the expression of dissenting views, it need not be turned into a trial-type adversarial proceeding with endless objections and cross-examination. Further, while a right of appeal from adoption of a plan may be appropriate to prevent officials from implementing discriminatory or factually baseless decisions, there is little reason to turn an appeal to a minister or a court into a full scale exercise of independent judgement on review. See Chapter III (d) supra. Because the officials designated in the law to prepare a land use plan have been designated because of their interest and expertise in matters related to land use, such expertise should be respected on appeal. Thus, it is appropriate to legislatively prescribe a limited scope of review on appeal which confines review to the administrative record and limits the reviewer to a determination of whether the decision being appealed is supported by any substantial evidence in the record. If it is, the law should provide for affirmance of the decision notwithstanding that the reviewer might have reached a different result had it exercised its independent judgement and thus re-weighed the evidence 121/.

2. Principles to Guide the Choice of a Recommended Land Use

Building a consensus about land use serves to overcome one aspect of the problem confronting planners when they are faced with the task of recommending a proposed land use. As we have noted, however, there is another aspect of the problem which legislation can help to solve; viz., the lack of substantive guidance in actually making a choice between competing alternative land uses. By establishing a set of carefully crafted, yet necessarily general guidelines, well drafted land use legislation can in fact serve two somewhat different purposes.

First, by establishing guides which actually direct the choice of a recommended land use in particular circumstances, land use planning principles will help to prevent the process of decision-making from bogging down. If planners and other decision-makers have a statutory matrix against which alternative land uses can be tested, then there is considerably less justification for flailing about and failing to produce a recommendation from among those alternatives. In this connection, of course, statutory planning principles become more useful as they become more specific. On the other hand,

---

121/ See Chapter III (d) supra; see also, for example, California Public Resources Code Section 21168 which precludes the exercise of independent judgement by courts reviewing administrative determinations made under the Environmental Quality Act. In addition see proposed Waters Enactment of Malaysia, Section 33 and Section 63 of proposed Water Resources Act, Samoa which also provide for limited review on appeal of administrative decisions made thereunder.

as they become more specific, principles become more narrow and thus less encompassing of the real life problems which may confront decision-makers. The trick then is to design statutory planning principles which are sufficiently specific to be instructive, without being so detailed that they are irrelevant to a large measure of the problems which are faced.

The other purpose served by planning principles is that they act as a statutory standard for judging the correctness - the legality - of the land use recommendation which is made. For instance, a principle may provide that where two or more alternative land uses are possible, it shall be the less water consumptive use which is selected. If, despite this principle, the decision-maker ignores one acceptable land use in favor of another which is much more consumptive of scarce water resources, there then exists a basis for saying that the decision is wrong; that, in fact, it is illegal. Statutory land use principles thus provide a means of identifying abuses of the decision-making power and, if connected to a right of appeal and review, the substantive legal basis for imposing a check upon such abuses.

Describing the benefits of a set of statutory planning principles is, not surprisingly, easier than listing the principles themselves. In part this is due to the fact that reasonable minds may differ over what constitutes an acceptable general planning principle or, if there is agreement about the principle, about how it should be expressed. Then too, planning principles are likely to be influenced by government policies or priorities regarding the use of land and are thus almost certain to vary from country to country or even region to region. Finally, planning principles are also likely to reflect the physical circumstances of the area in question - whether for instance the climate is dry or wet, whether there is abundant prime land, and so forth - and thus are subject to this additional variable.

Nonetheless, we believe there are certain general principles which are, or should be, universal in their application. Accordingly, in the material which follows we shall raise several of these for consideration. It should be understood of course that what is set forth is not intended to be a complete list. As noted, a variety of other principles specific to the circumstances at hand, may be appropriate. Moreover, we recognize that others may differ with us both about the inclusion of a particular principle and the way it is expressed.

a) Every Land Use Decision Should Take Into Account Not Only Benefits, But Also Direct and Secondary Costs, Including Non-Monetary Social and Environmental Costs Associated With the Decision

Anyone familiar with the development of large scale public works projects has probably encountered the term "cost-benefit analysis". The term arises from the United States where it has been enmeshed in water resources management for almost 50 years. The United States Flood Control Act of 1936 required *inter alia* that the benefits of any proposed flood control project must exceed costs for the project to be approved. Thus, use of the benefit-cost approach began with an effort to reduce project benefits and costs to monetary terms in order to allow their summation. A comparison of summed benefits and costs usually followed and resulted in the calculation of a cost/benefit "ratio". So long as the ratio exceeded the magical number of 1 - that is, so long as benefits exceeded costs - budget allocations for the project could be approved and work could commence.

Over time, use of the cost-benefit approach to determining project feasability spread beyond the field of water resources management and beyond the United States. As it did so, and as the cost-benefit ratio began to take on greater and greater importance to the determination of whether or not a proposed development project should proceed, a number of problems came to light. Among them were the fact that the process could be manipulated to produce results more or less "cooked" to order 122/; something which has been attributed, at least in part, to a lack of control of professional standards within the consulting industry 123/. In addition, for many years, the cost-benefit analysis, was seen as resting on a fairly narrow, monetary-based foundation : a reservoir would create X cubic meters of carryover storage sufficient to yield y bushels of maize having a value of Z dollars, for example. This was achieved at a cost of t hectares of land having a value of Q. If Z exceeded Q, the project was feasible. If the ratio of Z to Q exceeded similar ratios developed for alternatives to the reservoir, the reservoir was deemed to be relatively the best alternative.

Certainly, land use legislation is not a cure for all of these matters. Insofar as the problem of "cooked" results is concerned, for example, land use legislation is a rather inexact means of improving professional standards in the consulting industry, and we do not recommend that it be so used 124/. Consultant licensing, or even better, careful selection of

---

122/ Bennett and Thomas, in their excellent technical work on land use planning in Western Australia ("On Rational Grounds : Systems Analysis in Catchment Land Use Planning", Elsevier, 1982) quote an earlier writer who, after reviewing a study of some 200 cost-benefit analyses, said,

> "Someone once decried the fact that there were thousands of studies done for government agencies that were buried inthe executive branch files, and that they should all be revealed. I once believed that too, but now I think they probably should remain buried. The private contract research industry has been referred to as the "flimflam industry". I now understand the term".

"On Rational Grounds", p. 12.

123/ Ibid., Bennett and Thomas.

124/ For those who wish to pursue the subject nonetheless, we would recommend the Bennett and Thomas work cited above which, in turn refers, to a wealth of recent studies of the cost-benefit analysis approach, including : Peskin and Seskin, Compendium on Water Planning Economics; Tihansky's work on salinity damage cost for the U.S. Environmental Protection Agency; and the U.S. Bureau of Reclamation's Study of Salinity Control Programmes for the Colorado River.

consultants or training of local personnel, would appear to be of far greater utility. On the other hand, with regard to the problem of a narrow focus, it is our view that land use legislation can have value in broadening the foundation of the cost-benefit approach. Since the cost-benefit analysis - or more refined versions thereof, including calculations of internal rates of return - are likely to remain for sometime as one of the principal tools of determing relative project desireability, it is worth exploring this broadening impact a bit further.

As Bennett and Thomas 125/ note, the scope of the cost-benefit analysis began to enlarge in the 1960's to include systematic economic treatment of man-environmental relationships. Arising largely out of the problems of environmental pollution which had begun to receive vastly increased attention in the 1960's, one result of this enlargement was an attempt to quantify environmental effects within traditionally accepted investment criteria 126/. Another approach has sought to include non-monetary objectives as well as monetary ones in the design of projects 127/. Yet another approach attempts to classify - and thus emphasize - the differences between direct and secondary benefits and costs of proposed development alternatives. Under this approach, direct benefits or costs from a particular land use alternative are those that accrue to the user of the land in issue; revenue from crops, from the harvesting of timber, from the sale of meat or milk produced from grazing or the monetery costs of development are examples. Secondary benefits in turn are usually defined as the

---

125/ On Rational Grounds, supra.

126/ See Bennett and Thomas, p. 10 and cited studies. See also People ex.rel. Younger v. Superior Court 16 Cal.d 30 (1976) and San Francisco Civil Service Com. v. Superior Court 16 Cal.d 46 (1976) wherein the court grappled with the problem of valuing environmental costs for the purpose of awarding compensatory damages arising from pollution incidents.

127/ Ibid.

net benefits accruing to factors of production or consumers engaged in activities related to a development which would not have occurred in the absence of the project. Increased foreign exchange and lower unemployment are examples. Similarly, secondary costs may include indirect changes in the environment and the destruction of social systems.

What land use legislation can do is to assure that the cost-benefit equation includes secondary as well as direct benefits and costs in its calculations. It can also assure that non-monetary benefits and costs are "internalized" and not excluded from the cost-benefit calculation and thus passed on for another part of the government or the public to deal with. In short, it can promote a wider scope for the cost-benefit analysis and thus a truer picture of what are the real costs and benefits of series of development alternatives. It can do this by incorporating into any land use decision the principle that every such decision shall take into account not only project benefits but also direct and secondary costs including non-monetary social and environmental costs.

b) The Government Should Neither Implement, Fund the Implementation of nor Recommend the Implementation of a Particular Land Use Proposal Unless its Benefits Exceed its Direct and Secondary Costs

A corollary to the above discussed principle of considering the direct and secondary benefits and costs of each land use alternative, whether of a monetary or non-monetary character, is that no alternative should be implemented or recommended for implementation unless its projected benefits exceed its costs. In essence this is nothing more than a restatement of the basic cost-benefit rule. The nature of the restatement, however, is significant in that it incorporates the concept of the broadened cost benefit approach.

c) <u>Where Application of the Expanded Cost Benefit Analysis Methodology Shows Two or More Alternative land Uses to Be Justified, the Use Which is Less Socially and Environmentally Costly Will Be Preferred</u>

This principle goes to the heart of the selection process. In effect, it gives a "people" orientation to the land use decision-making process by directing decision makers toward alternatives which are less disruptive of people, their social and customary practices and their environment. Importantly, the principle applies only when there are two or more alternatives, <u>each</u> of which meets the cost-benefit analysis test. In otherwords, it does not promote an economically unacceptable alternative because it is more pleasing to the environmentalist or the sociologist. Nor does it provide that the more socially and environmentally costly alternative is infeasible. Instead, it simply - and quite properly - gives support to the notion that the land use planning process is more rational if it results in the selection of the least socially and environmentally harmful alternative from among several alternatives - all of which have an economically favorable cost-benefit ratio.

d) <u>That in Addition to Being Justified on Economic Grounds, Any Recommended Land Use Must be Reasonable in the Circumstances</u>

In the field of water resources management, it is common to refer to the concept of reasonable and beneficial use. Indeed, many modern statutory systems preclude the use of water unless the use is both reasonable <u>and</u> beneficial. Under these systems, the term "beneficial use" has tended to take on a meaning similar to the cost-benefit ratio. Does the use of water produce a net benefit, whether measured in monetary or non-monetary terms ? If so, the use is beneficial.

The term "reasonable use" on the other hand, has taken on a broader, more amorphous meaning. Essentially it asks whether, notwithstanding the economic or other benefit which a particular use of water may produce, is the use reasonable considering all of the circumstances ? As construed by the courts, reasonableness is a factual question and is to be determined on a case-by-case basis. Thus, what is a reasonable use of water may vary from location to location or even season to season depending upon the geographic or seasonal availability of water. Reasonableness may vary too depending upon the alternative uses which can be made of water and it may vary depending upon the effect of the proposed use upon others. Finally, it may change as the times change. Thus, for example, the transfer of water out of a basin for use elsewhere may have been reasonable 50 years ago when the basin of origin was relatively unpopulated; it may be unreasonable today after the basin of origin has experienced an influx of people.

While we recognize that the reasonableness concept has been limited until now to the water management field, we see no reason why it cannot and should not be applied to the field of land use planning as well. At heart, "reasonableness" is a common sense concept that, in essence, says notwithstanding favorable cost-benefit ratios and notwithstanding the eagerness of the project's proponents, is this something which, in view of all of the circumstances, a reasonable person of common understanding would support ? More frequently than one might expect, the answer is in the negative. Sometimes despite the fact that it is well oiled and full of fuel, the engine of development is just simply on the wrong road. The principle of "reasonableness" is intended to keep such erroneous excursions to a minimum.

e) No Person Has an Unalterable Right to a Particular Land Use and Government May Require the Alteration, Modification or Cessation of Any Particular Land Use When the Public Interest so Requires

Finally, we believe it is important to establish the primacy of the decision-maker in the land use planning process. Without a doubt it is important to involve the public in the process. Further, it is essential to consider non-monetary costs and social and environmental costs and benefits when weighing the relative desireability of different land use alternatives. Ultimately, however, the decision must be made. When the time comes, it frequently occurs that exceptional influence is brought to bear upon the decision-maker by those individuals or entities currently making use of the land. Such an occurrence is both predictable and entirely reasonable. Nor is it something to be ignored. As we have stated earlier, the building of a consensus, especially among those who use the land, is essential to the functioning of the land use planning process. Obviously the views of local users should be taken into account when making the planning decision about how "their" land should be used in the future.

There may be a time, however, when the interests of local land users and the larger public interest in the use of land irrevocably diverge. In such circumstances, it is important to make clear that it is the local interest which must give way. The statement of principle set forth above does that and, coincidentally, provides legal support for the decision-maker who faces the unpleasant task of placing the larger public interest ahead of local concerns. At the same time, the statement does not absolve Government of the responsibility to compensate local people for the subordination of their interest to the common good, if compensation is otherwise required under the law. In recent years, the issue of eminent domain has taken on considerable complexity as the use of planning tools has increased - a matter we describe in more detail in Chapter 7 under the heading of "Implementation". Because the law of eminent domain is in flux and varies considerably from jurisdiction to jurisdiction, in any event, it would be inappropriate for a general planning principle to speak to that issue. Accordingly, the principle set forth above is silent in this respect.

To summarize briefly, it is our view that guiding principles are useful in helping the decision-maker to select a recommended land use once the matching of land suitability determinations with land use requirements has produced a set of possible alternatives. To a significant degree, the principles which we have offered for this purpose are intended to keep the process from bogging down and, at the same time, to broaden the focus of the cost benefit methodology which will be applied to derive the alternative with the highest benefit to cost ratio. As we have attempted to describe, the selection of a most suitable land use alternative is not just a matter of numbers; it is a matter involving people and requiring a good measure of common sense. The principles set forth above, we hope, will tend to inject both into the decision-making process.

CHAPTER VII - THE EFFECTUATION OF LAND USE PLANS

An equitable, participatory and smoothly functioning land use planning mechanism is a major milestone on the road to more rational land use. By itself, however, even a process which fully meets the criteria discussed in preceding chapters will produce only a plan of proposed land uses. To actually achieve the policies and priorities that are represented in the plan, there must also exist a means of effectuation. In this chapter we shall discuss a variety of implementation measures which hypothetically could be used to achieve the intended results of a plan. As the conscientious reader might expect, the mix of these measures will vary considerably from case to case.

1. Legal Measures

To better convey the character of the measures which might be used to achieve the intended result of a land use plan, we have elected to use a classification scheme which divides those measures into two categories: legal and extra-legal. To briefly review the distinction drawn in the introductory chapter, legal measures are those exercised in accordance with statutory provisions that outline the extent of the measure and describe the manner of its exercise. They also frequently provide review procedures to forestal abuse. The exercise of regulatory power through the issuance or denial of development permits, development orders and zoning classifications as well as the exercise of eminent domain authority are examples of such legal measures.

Extra-legal measures, on the other hand, are land-use oriented programmes which - while usually possessing a basis in law - are not defined in such statutory detail nor so strictly controlled. Agricultural extension services, rural oriented training programmes and crop price supports are pertinent examples of such extra-legal measures.

In the material which follows, we shall examine a little more closely certain legal and extra-legal effectuation measures in order to explore their strengths and weaknesses. As we will see, while each may be intended to further the achievement of more rational land use, some measures may hold more promise for a developing country than others. Moreover, logic suggests, exclusive reliance upon one type of enforcement measure (legal, for example) may have less utility than an approach to implementation which employs both legal and extra-legal measures in combination. We turn to an examination of these issues.

a) The Link Between Land Use Plans and the Exercise of Regulatory Power

The exercise of legal regulatory measures in connection with the development of land serves little purpose if it is done in a random, *ad hoc* fashion. Rather, to attain the government's policy goals, there should exist a linkage between government's regulatory activities concerning land and an overall, comprehensive land use plan which inculcates those goals. If no such link exists not only will achievement of the government's policies be less likely; there may also be a corresponding increase in the risk of hapazard, arbitrary and -ultimately- abusive use of regulatory authority.

As early as 1914 when the first zoning enabling act was passed in the United States, it was realized that a comprehensive plan is an essential link between general regulatory objectives and regulations applicable to specific properties within each zoning district [128/]. Nor has time eroded the "essential" character of the connection. To the contrary, it has reinforced the bond between a general plan and specific regulatory action to the point that, in an increasing number of jurisdictions, the existence of the connection is a determinant of the legality of the exercise of regulatory power. The view expressed by the Oregon Supreme Court in this regard is typical :

128/ See Keene, "Farmland Protection" *supra* 15 Gonzaga Law Review 621 (1980).

> "In summary, we conclude that a comprehensive plan is the controlling land-use planning instrument for a city (or county). Upon passage of a comprehensive plan, a city (or county) assumes a responsibility to effectuate that plan and conform prior conflicting zoning ordinances to it. We further hold that the zoning decisions of a city (or county) must be in accord with that plan and a zoning ordinance which allows a more intensive use than that prescribed in the plan must fail." 129/

The reason such government regulatory activity must fail is that, legally speaking, it lacks a "rational basis". It achieves this dubious distinction by failing to conform to the provisions of a factually based plan of proposed land use, and thus is viewed as being without factual foundation. Without the proper factual underpinnings - and conformity to a general land use plan is increasingly viewed as an essential requisite for the proper underpinnings - government regulatory activity will be found to be without rational basis and thus, invalid. In sum, maintenance of a close linkage between the land use plan and government regulatory measures is important not only in the practical sense of encouraging land uses which will achieve the development policies woven into the land use planning document. It is also important in a legal context, since regulatory activity which is unconnected and non-conforming may well be held to be arbitrary and thus beyond government's power to maintain.

b) Development Permits and Development Orders

Given the legal and practical importance of a close connection between the land use plan and the exercise of government regulatory power over land, the question of how to create and maintain a relationship between the plan and the exercise of such power, naturally arises. One way is to channel

---

129/ Baker v. City of Milwaukie 533 P_2d 772, 779 (1975).

the exercise of regulatory power through a system of development permits which are themselves linked to the specific proposals contained in a relevant land use plan.

Such an approach to implementation has been followed in Malaysia through adoption of the Town and Country Planning Act, 1976. There, a State Planning Committee is established for each of the country's 13 states and is given the task of promoting the conservation, use and development of all lands in the State, within the framework of the national policy 130/. In fact, however, the law makes the State Authority responsible mainly for generally directing and coordinating various local planning authorities which are given the bulk of the responsibility for actual on-the-ground planning work 131/. Within its area, each local planning authority is responsible for data collection and for regulating, controlling and planning the development and use of all lands and buildings within its area 132/. Under the provisions of the Act, it is expected to exert such control through a process encompassing several sequential steps.

First, each local authority is expected to undertake a survey of its area, including physical, social, economic and environmental characteristics; the size, composition and distribution of population; and the communications and transport systems and traffic of the area, among others 133/. Second,

---

130/ Malaysia, Town and Country Planning Act, Sec. 4. The Act does not set forth the National Policy except to declare that the State Authority "shall be responsible for the general policy in respect of the planning of the development and use of all lands and buildings within the area of every local authority in the State." Ibid., Sec. 3.

131/ The multi-layered planning responsibility set forth in the Malaysia law is a good indicator of the practical impact of the necessity of changing scale from global to local in order to produce useful plans. it indicates as well the importance of derising a statutory mechamism which provides for a smooth transition between levels (and scale of plans).

132/ Malaysia Town and Country Planning Act, Sec. 6.

133/ Ibid., Sec. 7.

each authority is expected to prepare and submit to the State Planning Authority for review, a draft structure plan which, inter alia, formulates the general proposals of the local planning authority regarding the developmentand use of land within its area 134/. Once the local plan has been submitted to the State Planning Committee and been approved 135/, it takes effect.

It is the law's directive that the local plan shall "come into effect" 136/ which brings the Malaysia legislation within the ambit of this chapter on implementation. What exactly does the phrase "come into effect" mean ? Under the Malaysia legislation it means quite simply that once the local plan is approved,

> "No person shall use or permit to be used any land or building otherwise than in conformity with the local plan". 137/.

In sum, the plan becomes binding upon those who use, or propose to use, land covered by the plan. Regulatory control to implement this binding character of the plan is then provided through the granting of a "planning permission" - in substance, a development permit. Section 19 of the law provides that, except for certain activities having minor impact 138/,

---

134/ Malaysia Town and Country Planning Act, Sec. 8. The law also provides for ample public participation while such structure plans are being prepared at the local level.

135/ The Malaysia law provides a variety of safeguards for insuring that approval will not be given until any objections to the contents of the draft structure plan have been heard and considered.

136/ Malaysia Town and Country Planning Act, Sec. 10.

137/ Ibid., Sec. 18.

138/ Such activities include : 1) minor alterations to existing buildings, 2) excavations, including wells made in the ordinary course of agricultural operations in areas zoned for agriculture and 3) the use of any land or building for a period not in excess of one month. Sec. 19 (2).

"No person, other than a local authority shall commence, undertake or carry out any development unless planning permission in respect to the development has been given to him."

Further, no person may undertake or carry out any proposed development _except_ in conformity with the planning permission that is granted [139/]. Under the Malaysia law, "planning permission" must be applied for by formal application made to the local planning authority [140/]. In dealing with the application, the local planning authority is, in turn, required to "take into consideration" the provisions of the development plan it has prepared or is in the process of preparing [141/]. If such consideration reveals that the proposed development will contravene any provision of the development plan, then the law _requires_ that the local authority deny planning permission [142/].

The "planning permission" thus provided for by the Malaysia Town and Country Planning Act - like most development permit schemes - is a precondition to the right to engage in the use or development of land. Moreover, the permission is also the measure of the right. A planning permission does not authorize unrestricted use; to the contrary, it authorizes development only as prescribed in the permission itself and usually provides for revocation of the right if the terms of the permission are exceeded. Finally, as seen, the planning permission is grounded upon a development plan. That plan must be taken into consideration when a development application is reviewed and no permission may be granted if the development contravenes the local plan. In sum, the Malaysia law provides for vertically integrated plan development and also for the recommended close connection or linkage between the planning process and plan implementation.

139/ Malaysia Town and Country Planning Act, Sec. 21.

140/ _Ibid._, Sec. 21.

141/ _Ibid._, Sec. 22.

142/ _Ibid._

A different approach to implementation is contained in the Agriculture Act of Kenya 143/. Rather than exerting regulatory control over applications to develop land as does the Malaysia law, Kenya's legislation authorizes government ordered implementation of a "land development programme". Whenever a local (district) agricultural committee concludes that the proper development of land for agricultural purposes or the interests of good land management require, it may recommend to the country's Central Agricultural Board that a land development order be issued with respect to particular lands 144/. If the Central Board accepts the recommendation, it serves a notice upon the owner or occupier of the land in question, which notice requires the submission of a "development programme" in respect of such lands. Failing the submission of such a programme, the Central Board is directed to prepare a programme itself. And to what does such a "programme" refer ? According to the law, it means,

> "the adoption of such a system of management or farming practices or other system in relation to the land in question (including the execution of such work and the placing of such things in, on or over the land, from time to time) as the Central Agricultural Board may consider necessary for the proper development of the land for agricultural purposes 145/."

Thus, while not a formal land use "plan", the "development programme" is nonetheless intended as a coherent centrally authorized approach to rural agrarian land development.

143/ Kenya Agriculture Act (1980).

144/ Agriculture Act of Kenya, Sec. 65.

145/ *Ibid.*, Sec. 64 (3).

Where a proposed land development programme is received and approved by the Central Board or where the Board itself devises the programme, it then makes a land development order against the owner or occupier of the land in issue 146/. Subject to certain procedural safeguards, such an order is binding upon the owner or occupier who is obliged to complete the development programme approved by the Central Board 147/. Over time, through the making an enforcing of a series of such orders, a government-directed pattern of land use emerges.

The Malaysia and Kenyan laws thus represent approaches to implementation which proceed in the opposite direction but reach the same result - a pattern of planned land uses implemented through regulatory control. By analogue, they can be compared with the mechanics of deduction and induction. In the case of the former, reasoning proceeds from a stated premise (for example, a plan) to draw various conclusions (specific applications). The Malaysia Town and Country Planning Act follows such an approach. In the latter case, reasoning proceeds from a series of applications (in our case, individual development orders) to yield a general conclusion (in our case, an overall plan of development). The Agriculture Act of Kenya is such an example. Inasmuch as both approaches yield a similar result; i.e., the implementation of planned development, each would appear to be valid.

c) Zoning Classifications

Earlier we noted that, in some jurisdictions, a close connection between a comprehensive land use plan and zoning classifications is an enforceable legal requirement. Failure to observe that requirement, we noted, could invalidate a government's regulatory action regarding land. In other jurisdictions the connection, while perhaps not so rigorously enforced by the judiciary, nonetheless is evident in efforts to control land development through the establishment of zones.

146/ Agriculture Act of Kenya, Sec. 48.

147/ Ibid., Sec. 73.

In Uruguay, for example, Act No. 13.667 (1968) concerning soil and water conservation provides for the establishment of soil conservation "regions" throughout the country 148/. Each such region is intended to be,

> "a geographical area with boundaries defined by the Ministry of Agriculture in such a way that an integrated approach is taken to soil conservation in areas where soils are used in such a manner that damage is likely to result or has already occurred from erosion or improper soil use and thus calls for immediate action." 149/.

Within such regions, the Act then provides for the initiation of soil conservation programmes which, it appears, are to be carried forward in accordance with a Soil and Water Conservation Plan established by resolution. Each such Plan is required to identify the property or area affected by soil problems, the proposed works to be carried out and, the practices to be followed by farmers participating in the programme 150/. In short, the designation of the zone (region) serves to focus the conservation effort on a particular geographic area. Within such area, specific activities (the programme) are linked to a plan which more generally describes the works and practices to be undertaken throughout the zone.

Apart from its illustration of the linkage which exists between plans and specific land use activities, the Uruguay law is also helpful in demonstrating how zoning controls work. Frequently, zoning is the end product of the planning process. As a means of expressing their intention to carry forward government land use policies, planners may identify certain areas (zones) where activities such as agriculture will be encouraged, in part through the suppression of competing activities such as residential

---

148/ Uruguay Act No. 13.667, Sec. 7.

149/ *Ibid*.

150/ *Ibid*., Sec. 9.

development. As the Uruguay example indicates, the zone is normally not created until government has <u>already</u> done its basic planning work - in the case of Uruguay, the planning is needed to identify soil erosion as a national problem.

As the example also indicates, the creation of a zone is not <u>per se</u> enough to bring about the desired land use result. Simply creating a soil conservation zone (or an agricultural zone, or a commercial or industrial zone) means little unless the law also fleshes out such a designation by detailing the characteristics of each classification. In Uruguay, for example, the designation of a soil conservation region legislatively carries with it the legal determination that the region is an area where land is used in a manner which has created or will create erosion problems, that farming practices within the region can be controlled and, that corrective measures can and will be carried out. Similarly, a zoning classification of land as "agricultural" means little unless the law goes on to provide that any land so classified may not, for example, be the site of residential or commercial structures or that such structures, if built, may not exceed a certain density per hectare or that lands so designated may be used to grow only certain crops, and so on.

The presence of such limitations, while necessary for the functioning of a zoning law, also gives rise to another important issue that may confront regulators when they use zoning controls to implement their land use plans. The issue is whether the application of such controls results in a taking of property that requires compensation.

Not infrequently, zoning restrictions result in a substantial diminution in the value of the property to which they are applied [151/]. Land which could be used for commercial or residential purposes as well as agricultural purposes, will simply not have as high a market value if a zoning measure is imposed which limits use exclusively to agriculture or which

---

151/ See Keene, <u>Farmland Protection : Legal and Constitutional Issues</u>, 15 Gonzague Law Review, 621 (1980).

requires large minimum lot sizes. If government has to provide compensation to land owners for the reduction in market value brought about by such measures it could, in effect, be compelled to "buy" the right to regulate land use. The result may be a failure by cash-poor governments to regulate land use practices even when such regulation is essential to prevent long-term damage to the land 152/.

Unfortunately, the existing legislation of many developing countries provides little help in resolving the question of whether government is obliged to compensate land owners whose lands are subjected to zoning limitations. Much existing legislation provides for the payment of compensation to landowners 153/. Rarely, if ever however, does it speak to the question of the obligation to provide compensation as a result of the imposition of zoning restrictions. As a result, it has often been left to the courts to determine the existence and scope of such an obligation. Generally speaking it is the courts of the more developed countries which have confronted such questions in connection with invese condemnation litigation brought to recover the decrease in market value caused by government regulation of the use of land. As noted earlier in this work, the trend of decisions in such cases is away from requiring compensation where government

---

152/ Such a situation has in fact arisen in Western Samoa. There, customary practices regarding land ownership have led to an increase in the clearing of natural vegetation in order to plant taro - a crop which depletes the soil. So extensive has this practice become that a number of important watersheds have been threatened with destruction. Although Government pocesses the legal authority to zone watershed reserve areas (Forests Act, Secs. 59-62) any effort to do so has been met with numerous claims for compensation. The result is that in the nearly 20 years such authority has existed, it has only been exercised to create one such reserve.

153/ See, e.g., the Lesotho Land Act (1979), Secs. 54-56; Kenya Agriculture Act, Sec. 61; Samoa Taking of Lands Act (1964), Sec. 25; Botswana National Water Resources Act; Congo Land Code (1983), Secs. 22-25.

regulation simply reduces the value of land. instead, in an effort to balance property rights with the need for government to regulate land use in appropriate circumstances, courts in the leading jurisdictions have held that the obligation of government to provide compensation exists only when regulatory action eliminates all possible use. A mere reduction in value resulting from a change in zoning from commercial to agricultural or a reduction in value caused by a zoning change increasing minimum lot sizes thus does not require compensation if some productive use can still be made.

Litigation thus provides an answer to the question of compensation. Litigation is also, however, expensive, time consuming and uncertain. Thus, it is immeasurably better to protect government's efforts to implement its land use plans through zoning, by anticipating potential compensation claims and providing guidance as to when such claims may be maintained and when they may not. A statutory provision which incorporates the gist of the court decisions described above would, in our view, do much to give government the confidence to utilize land-use controls to implement its plans while at the same time protecting the public from overreaching government regulation.

d) The Assertion of Public Trust Authority

A still-emerging concept that holds promise for the implementation of land-use plans is the assertion of public trust authority to prevent the destruction of land and water sources necessary to satisfy public needs. The core of the doctrine is the state's authority as sovereign to exercise continuous supervision and control over the navigable waters of the state and the lands underlying those waters [154/]. The doctrine may extend as well to the protection of watershed lands necessary to ensure a plentiful supply of water for agricultural and other broad public purposes.

154/ National Audubon Society v. Superior Court Supreme Court of California No. S.F. 24368 (1983).

In essence the doctrine is this : as the sovereign power, government holds in trust for all of the people those lands which are essential to the well being of all of the people. Even if those lands are conveyed to private persons for use, they are conveyed subject to the public trust. Thus, if the lands underlie an important river or harbor, they cannot be filled and built upon if doing so would deprive the people of a public asset important to their common well being. Similarly, if certain lands serve as part of a watershed that is an essential source of freshwater for the public, then the public trust authority may be exercised - even if the lands are privately held - to prevent development which will jeopardize the public trust values of those lands.

The roots of the doctrine arise from Roman law. According to Justinian,

> "By the law of nature these things are common to mankind - the air, running water, the sea and consequently the shores of the sea." 155/

From this origin, the English common law evolved the concept of the public trust, under which the sovereign owns "all of its navigable waterways and the lands lying beneath them 156/.

Originally directed at the protection of navigation, commerce and fisheries, the objectives of the public trust have evolved in tandem with the changing public perception of the use of waterways. As a result, those jurisdictions which have directly considered the doctrine have found it sufficiently flexible to encompass changing public needs. Thus, for instance, the doctrine has been used to preserve tidal lands in their natural state

---

155/ Institutes of Justinian 2.1.1.

156/ Spanish law and, subsequently, Mexican law have also recognized the public trust doctrine.

so that they may serve as ecological units for scientific study, as open space and as environments which provide food and habitat for birds and marine life [157/]. Since watershed lands also serve the public need of providing a source of supply for agriculture and domestic needs, it would logically seem that the doctrine could - and should - be sufficiently flexible to provide for the protection of such lands so that they may continue to serve these functions. Accordingly,the public trust doctrine emerges - especially in jurisdictions where the rule of law is based upon the English system - as an alternative means of regulating land use so as to achieve planning purposes.

But why consider the public trust when other more direct mechanisms are available ? The answer relates in part to the subject of compensation just discussed. The public trust doctrine is an attribute of sovereignty. It exists from the very fact that there is a sovereign and need not be created by statute. Thus, the public trust pre-dates the distribution of land to private owners, and such distribution is consequently made subject to the public trust. For this reason, it is more difficult for private owners to claim a vested right to develop land contrary to public trust values. Accordingly, even if the trust has remained dormant for years or decades, Government can assert it if needed to stop development which will interfere with trust purposes. Moreover, it can assert the trust without having to compensate land owners against whom the trust is asserted. This is so, since land is held subject to the public trust, thus precluding the acquisition of a compensable vested right that can be asserted against trust values.

In sum, providing in land use legislation that government may continue to assert the public trust in order to protect the public value of water sources and water related lands, is another potentially useful way of giving government the means of implementing the policies contained in a land use plan.

157/ Audubon Society v. Superior Court, *supra*, p. 24.

e) Acquisition of Ownership Interests

Perhaps the most direct way to control land use is through expropriation. Frequently efforts to reform land tenure will focus uon a particular geographic region and centre around the acquisition of land from one group of owners with subsequent redistribution to another group.

In Peru, for instance, the purpose of the Land Reform Act (1969) is to replace a scheme of very large landholdings (latifundios) and very small holdings (minifundios) by a more equitable system of land ownership and tenancy that will increase output and productivity as well as raise farm incomes [158/]. To accomplish this goal, the Act first declares the expropriation of privately owned rural holdings to be in the public interest. It then makes all idle or inefficiently worked land and all land which is excessively large or small and is worked by tenants [159/], subject to its provisions. Following preparation of a plan for bringing land under the Act [160/], every owner of land within each land reform zone is notified of adoption of the Plan and is informed of the valuation made of the area subjected to the Act, the form of payment and the amount of compensation to be paid (Article 52). The government may then obtain an order of immediate possession. Following resolution of any argument about compensation, a deed is made over and the government enters into formal ownership of the land in question. According to the law, no legal action may "obstruct, postpone or paralyze" the expropriation procedure [161/]. Thereafter, once its title

---

158/ Peru, Land Reform Act (Act No. 17.716).

159/ What is excessively large or small is based upon the concept of a "family agricultural unit" which is to be determined for each agrarian reform zone.

160/ The plan for bringing land under the Act is first prepared in draft, then revised in light of a field inspection, then noticed to the public, then made subject to the observations of the land owners (Art. 50). An administrative body known as a Zonal Directorate rules on any observations, obligations or requests which are made (*Ibid.*). Following the resolution of any appeals from such rulings, a final plan for bringing land under the Act is approved and published (*Ibid.*).

161/ *Ibid.*, Art. 59.

to the expropriated land is secure, the Government's Department of Land Reform and Land Settlement undertakes to allocate the land to rural inhabitants who have no land or who own an insufficient amount of land for farming 162/. Peasant Communities and cooperatives also enjoy a preference to the land to be allocated.

Nor is land reform the sole rationale for government's utilization of the spending power to acquire land. In Uruguay, for example, the Government, upon request of the Ministry of Agriculture, may acquire any land situated within a soil and water conservation region which has been seriously damaged by continuously worsening erosion and which cannot be reclaimed by private individuals by reason of the magnitude of the works involved 163/.

Further, it is increasingly clear that government need not purchase the entire fee simple interest in land in order to direct development. Rather, it may purchase the owner's "development rights". In essence this means determining the difference in the market value of the land if it is used for agricultural purposes and the higher market value which would obtain if the land was used for residential, commercial or industrial development. If government pays this difference, it buys (and thus controls) the non-agricultural development rights while the owner remains in physical possession of the right to work the land for agricultural purposes. As of 1984, six states of the United States had enacted such legislation authorizing state agencies or local government to acquire less than fee interest in land for the purpose of preserving prime agricultural property 164/.

162/ Ibid., Art. 66.

163/ Uruguay, Act No. 13.667 declaring soil and water conservation to be in the national interest. Sec. 12.

164/ New Jersey, Maryland, Massachusetts, Connecticut, Rhode Island and New Hampshire. See Keene, Farmland Protection : Legal and Constitutional Issues, 15 Gonzaga Law Review 621; See also, Netherton, Environmental Conservation and Historic Preservation through Recorded Land-Use Agreements. 14 Real Ppty Prob and Tru. J. 540580 (1979).

Finally, in a manner akin to the purchase of an interest in land, some governments have received statutory authorization to contract with landowners regarding the use of land for a specific period of time. Typically, these contracts concern agricultural land which is located on the periphery of urban development and is thus subject to market value escalation as development moves closer. In essence the agreements provide that government will agree to tax the land as agricultural land, rather than at a value which reflects its "highest and best" use, which may be for residential, commercial or industrial purposes. In return, the owner agrees to keep his land in agricultural use for a specified period of time - typically 10 to 15 years [165]. By agreeing to a lower tax take from the land, government, in effect, "buys" the contractual right to keep the land in agricultural production for a limited period of time. Coincidentally, it achieves the benefit of increased food production and a barrier to uncontrolled urban expansion [166].

2. Extra-legal Measures

Considerable variety also exists in the extra-legal measures available to effectuate land use decisions. If these measures are given a statutory basis through incorporation into land use planning legislation their use may be encouraged.

a) Extension Services

The stepchild of agrarian development in many countries is the government's extension programme. Frequently understaffed and almost always underfunded, the extension divisions of many departments of agriculture are

---

165/ See, e.g., the Williamson Act, California Public Resources Code.

166/ Unfortunately, such legislation has not been entirely free from problems. Often, it includes a provision which relieves the landowner of his obligations if he can produce evidence that keeping his land in continued agricultural production for the remainder of the agreed-upon time period will produce unanticipated hardship. See e.g. California Public Resources Code. Occasionally this provision has been invoked by landowners who have reaped the benefit of a lower tax rate and wish to sell when the right buyer comes along. The result, predictably, has been litigation.

often operated as an after thought to other agrarian programmes. As such they present, in our view, one of the underutilized opportunities to implement the government's agrarian development plans.

Throughout this work we have stressed the importance of building a consensus about the use of land. The provision of extension services is one of the surest ways of building such a consensus. First, extension activities are one of the few ways government has to reach the lowest level of land use decision making, viz. the land user. Moreover, extension services represent an example of government giving, rather than government taking. They provide knowledge, tools, seeds and fertilizers rather than taxes, expropriations, orders and controls. Finally, they are delivered in terms that the land user can understand. Farmers, particularly, are among the most practical of people; indeed, nature dictates that they must be if they are to survive the onslaughts of weather, pests and government. By the same token, extension activities work because they provide practical advice. They educate the farmer on the ground, in the field, about better techniques of ploughing, planting and cultivating. Moreover, if done properly, they can demonstrate through pilot plots exactly how yields (and thus income) will increase if certain techniques are followed.

Why then, given these tangible benefits, extension programmes tend to be treated badly is unclear. Whatever the cause, the drafting of land use legislation provides an opportunity to rectify this situation by directing that the talents of extension personnel be put to work to implement the government's land use policies. Legislation recently drafted for Western Samoa suggests one way in which this can be done [167/]. At the present time, Samoa's water resources are under attack, chiefly from development in the country's important watersheds. Natural vegetation is being cleared and replaced with taro - a crop notorious for its propensity to deplete the soil. After two or three years of planting, the soil is depleted and agriculture moves on. What remains is land relatively incapable of holding a vegetation cover. The end result then, is a watershed with reduced water retention (and thus water production) capability.

167/ FAO, Assistance in Water Legislation (1984) RAS/79/123.

In these circumstances, FAO has drafted legislation, at government request, which largely relies in part upon extension personnel to produce a favorable resolution of the situation 168/. That legislation first creates a National Water Resources Board and directs it to prepare a water resources master plan which includes designated watershed protection "zones" and related regulatory controls on development within such zones. It then goes on to provide :

> "When the National Water Resources Board has created a watershed protection zone, through the National Water Resources Plan or otherwise, any landowner or village affected thereby, shall be entitled to assistance from the Extension Division of the Department of Agriculture, Forestry and Fisheries on a priority basis. Upon a request from an affected village or landowner... the Extension Division shall meet with and advise the landowner or village fono [council] concerning crops and farming practices, including the construction of access roads and the application of chemicals which are compatible with the purposes of the watershed protection zone." 169/.

In sum, the legislation obliges government to make use of its extension division to provide on the ground assistance which will convince, rather than compel, farmers to change their practices. By so doing, it is hoped that the extension division will contribute to the consensus that is essential for any land use plan to work.

b) The Training of Personnel

The training of personnel and the conduct of crop research and other programmes are other important extra-legal contributors to rural development. Personnel training, in particular, may be essential to the long term

---

168/ See Wilkinson, Report and Proposal for National Water Resources Legislation for Samoa, FAO Project RTAS/79/123 (1984).

169/ Draft National Water Resources Act for Samoa, Sec. 56.

implementation of the government's policy goals. Knowledge about how to collect and properly massage natural resource data-inputs is critical to the preparation of a land use plan. If a country's officials lack such knowledge, then it must be obtained either through training or the provision of expert consultants who already possess the necessary skills. We do not, however, believe that the use of consultants over the long term is desireable; *inter alia* it creates a perpetual dependancy upon their services and stunts development of the country's own capabilities. To avoid such a dependency it may be provided, by law, that the employment of experts in land use planning techniques shall be upon the condition that each such expert works with a local counterpart. Further it may be provided that as part of the bargained-for expertise, the counterpart shall be trained in the expert's particular skill.

c) Government Pricing of Agricultural Products

Often government pursues a particular pricing policy with regard to agricultural products. It may, for instance, desire the production of crops capable of being exported and earning foreign exchange. Accordingly, where government is capable of influencing the market price paid for agricultural products it will do so to further its goals. Occasionally, however, government's desire to achieve a certain end result may cause it to use means which ultimately threaten attainment of the objective. One example is when government marketing boards suppress the price paid to farmers for a particular crop in order to maximize government revenue from sales of the crop on world markets. At some price level farmers will refuse to produce the crop simply because their revenues fail to meet expenses.

To prevent government overreaching in this regard, it is worthwhile to consider the inclusion in land use legislation of a provision that government marketing boards who purchase agricultural products grown in accordance with the directives of any land use plan, shall set a price sufficiently high to encourage *continued* production in accordance with the plan. Such a provision would change the criteria used to measure the marketing boards' performance and might thereby increase their collective horizons so as to encompass more than short-term profit.

CHAPTER VIII - THE MONITORING AND ENFORCEMENT OF LAND USE PLANS

Once land use plan implementation has begun, the issue of compliance comes to the fore. Even if the plannning process produces one or more land-use plans that are thoughtfully prepared, and even if government seeks to implement those plans through appropriate legal or extra-legal means, only a reliable monitoring mechanism well disclose whether the planning effort works, is defective in some respect or is being ignored. If it is the latter, then the question of appropriate enforcement must also be considered.

1) Monitoring

Feedback is important to the functioning of any regulatory process, including land use planning. Without it, mistakes in planning or implementation are more likely to remain undetected and thus uncorrected. Similarly, efforts to circumvent a plan or related implementation measures will be more difficult to uncover and to stop if feedback about compliance is unavailable.

In these circumstances, it is odd that the subject of compliance monitoring is rarely dealt with in land development or other natural resources legislation. Instead, such legislation typically leaps from a statement of authorized implementation measures, to a declaration of civil and criminal penalties in the event such measures are violated, without benefit of the bridge provided by a programme of monitoring. Perhaps the lack of legislation is why monitoring is frequently the weakest link in the chain of natural resources management.

Because compliance monitoring is normally not found in land development legislation and because those monitoring mechanisms which do exist are usually weak in any event, the subject of monitoring presents the lawyer or planner with another opportunity to improve the development process. To take full advantage of this opportunity, however, it is important that attention be paid to several elements usually found in those monitoring programmes which work. In our view these elements are the following :

- a clearly stated reason for monitoring;
- a monitoring mechanism which is practical;
- a monitoring process which is consistent; and
- a right of access for monitoring purposes which is unequivocal.

In the material which follows, we shall briefly discuss these elements in order to show how each contributes to the provision of reliable feedback.

a) A Clearly Stated Reason for Monitoring

Monitoring compliance with natural resources legislation is boring. It involves a lot of looking, testing, walking and form filling. It is at the opposite pole from policy making and it is work performed under conditions that are frequently unpleasant and sometimes hazardous. It thus is not surprising that the people who do monitoring work sometimes lose a sense of direction and ask what the purpose is and whether that purpose is worth the effort.

Certainly legislation is not a panacea for all of the problems endemic in such repetitive and sometimes tedious work. It can, however, serve to provide a sense of direction which may act as a reference point when monitoring personnel begin to question the value of their work. It can do this through a statutory statement that explains as clearly as possible <u>why</u> compliance monitoring is important and <u>how</u> monitoring fits as an integral part of the entire land use development process. In this connection, the words "why" and "how" are especially important - and thus have been emphasized in the preceding sentence. In our view, it is neither sufficient, nor desireable, to simply draft a statement which exhorts monitoring personnel to do their best for the betterment of the common good. Such a statement explains nothing and is likely to be perceived as a propaganda pronouncement. It is far better, in our view, to take more time and care in drafting a statement of purpose which explains rather than remonstrates. Not only are monitoring personnel likely to respond more positively to statutory language which deals thoughtfully with their concerns; the lawyer is also likely to find the drafting of a monitoring programme easier when it proceeds from a clear statement of purpose.

b) A Monitoring Mechanism Which Is Practical

It cannot be overemphasized that in order for it to succeed at its purpose, a compliance monitoring mechanism must be practical. Developing countries do not usually have barrels of cash sitting around waiting to be spent on personnel (including vehicles and petrol) designated in legislation as some kind of monitoring team. Rather, the reality is that such countries are short of personnel, short of vehicles and usually desperately short of petrol and the cash with which to buy it. What this means in practice is that a monitoring mechanism must, to the maxium extent feasible, rely upon people who can assist in monitoring compliance as part of the other duties for which they are responsible. But what does that mean ?

It means to a considerable extent reaping the fruits of a planning process which incorporates the principle of consensus; one of the reasons we have emphasized the concept so much. If a planning decision is reached by consensus (or if the consensus is otherwise taken into account) there will be people with a stake in the decision. Quite naturally these people will have an interest in seeing that the decision is carried out and is not ignored or violated. Not infrequently such people will be represented on the interdisciplinary planning body which makes the planning decision that is to be monitored. Sometimes they will be the land users at whom the decision is directed. The point is that there is - or should be if the planning process is working properly - a constituency for every planning decision which is made. If there is not, the decision itself should be investigated to determine why it was reached.

In these circumstances, it is not unreasonable to direct that monitoring of compliance with a particular planning decision shall be the responsibility of the people intended to benefit from it. They, after all, will have the incentive to monitor compliance; indeed, compared with the benefits to be provided by a particular decision, the cost to such persons of monitoring may be relatively small. It is fair to ask, nonetheless, how legislation can achieve such a result.

One way a competent monitoring programme can be mounted is to provide that, under the coordination of one person responsible to an interdisciplinary planning body, each government department or other entity represented on the body shall be responsible for monitoring any land related activity which may affect their own area of responsibility. At least in a vague way, government departments are generally aware of activities which may cause them difficulty. Thus, if the relevant planning body is broadly interdisciplinary - as it should be - a statutory provision which makes each member of the board responsible for monitoring (with central coordination of course) may well generate a fairly broad monitoring effort. This is especially so if the central coordinator, or his superiors, are authorized to take action to protect from infringement the interests of those entitites represented on the planning body.

Where the concept of consensus in planning extends to the local level - as it also should - it may be feasible to include local land users within the monitoring efforts. This is especially so where customary ways are strong and land use development legislation respects rather than obliterates such ways. Generally, we have found, where customary practices are strong, people tend to be vigilant and protective of their rights. If such rights can be combined with an interest in the benefits of a land use plan, a workable, local system of monitoring may be possible to develop - if it is tied to customary means of enforcement [170/].

170/ If local monitoring means turning one's neighbor over to the authorities for punishment under a western system of law, a locally based monitoring system may not function as well.

c) A Monitoring Process Which Is Consistent

For it to work effectively, compliance monitoring should also be consistent, especially where scientific testing is involved (as in the evaluation of wastewater effluent, for example). In essence, monitoring involves repeated comparisons of observed phenomena with a known standard. The regularity of such observations tends to ensure their objectivity. Thus, monthly observations of rainfed agricultural properties made throughout the year would tend to disclose springtime incursions by nomadic herders. Observations made only in the summer would show nothing. Similarly, weekly testing of surface water sources - done whether it rains or shines - might disclose high levels of fecal coliform or phosphate pollution carried by rainwater runoff from particular properties. The same testing carried out only when it was warm and dry would reveal very little.

Accordingly, where legislation is directed at the subject of compliance monitoring, we believe it is useful to specify that any observations or testing undertaken as a part of such monitoring should be conducted at regular intervals. The sole exception to such a provision might be where there is an express determination that irregular observations or testing are sufficient in the circumstances and that regular observations or testing will provide no additional benefits.

d) An Unequivocal Right of Access for Monitoring Purposes

One of the major problems facing compliance monitoring programmes throughout the world, is that of gaining access to the property to be monitored. People do not like intrusions upon their property - especially by government officials. This natural dislike tends to be heightened if the owner or occupier of land believes the official will find something he shouldn't. The result is that officials engaged in monitoring may meet locked gates, angry animals or even armed citiznes all of whom may serve to increase the excitement of the monitoring job - and probably act to keep it from being accomplished.

In these circumstances, government is often hesitant to proceed with the monitoring, not because it lacks the physical means to overcome such obstacles, but because is unsure of its legal ground for doing so. Increasingly, governments have become liability-conscious and the possibility of liability for a decision to act - whether the liability is fiscal or political - may cause a government to falter on the question of access for monitoring purposes. Thus the problem of access can bring to a standstill a compliance monitoring programme which is otherwise well conceived.

Land use legislation which deals with the subject of compliance monitoring can quickly firm up the legal ground for access by clearly according to any official engaged in monitoring, the right of access to private property for the purpose of ascertaining compliance with the provisions of any land use development plan or related permit. If prevailing religious or customary practices or common sense requires that such access be limited to certain hours, that also can be provided. Finally, the legislation could require as well that any official engaged in monitoring shall be provided with official written authorization to that effect. Not only would such a provision curtail abuse of the access priviledge, it might also persuade otherwise reluctant owners or occupiers to grant entry.

To sum up, the above suggestions will not of themselves, of course, eliminate confrontations between owners and occupiers of land and officials seeking to ascertain compliance with relevant land use requirements. They will, however, provide government with a legal basis that minimizes exposure to liability and thus encourages performance of the monitoring obligation.

2. Enforcement

In contrast to compliance monitoring language, enforcement provisions - particularly civil fines and criminal penalties - are almost always present in the law of most developing countries. The question we usually ask about these sometimes draconian measures, however, is how often are they used. The answer typically received is almost never.

While civil and criminal penalties for non-compliance have their place, we are increasingly inclined to view them as measures to be used as a last resort when other techniques of dispute resolution have failed. In part this view stems from the origin of the typical civil or cirminal provision. Generally speaking such measures have their source in the statutory language of a western law and have been grafted onto the legislation of the developing country. Frequently, in fact, these enforcement remedies are part of old, colonial legislation or can be traced to such legislation.

Western law, however, rests on a socio/juridical base that is often far different from the legal and social traditions encountered in a society which functions according to custom. A prison sentence, for example, tends to be a western idea. Arbitration, discussion among local rulers, payment of compensation in kind and retribution ("pay back", if you will) are more prevalent forms of dispute resolution and punishment in many developing countries.

Because of the paucity of use of westernized civil and criminal penalties as well as the availability of traditional remedies we are increasingly inclined to draft legislation which utilizes traditional enforcement mechanisms - at least in those situations where customary practices can give adequate relief. Where customary practices are not adequate - for instance where the violator of a plan, permit or license is a commercial or industrial enterprise - the westernized enforcement mechanism may still be appropriate. Thus, for example, in Samoa where a well developed system of customary law still exhibits great strength, FAO has proposed natural resources legislation which attempts to use customary practices to resolve disputes and violations of the law occuring on customary lands [171/]. Only if the use of such customary procedures fails to resolve the controversy are such western concepts as injunctive relief, monetary fines and jail terms, to be used.

171/ FAO draft Water Resources Act for Samoa (1985). Secs. 58 and 62.

In short, the key word concerning enforcement is the word "appropriate". If the enforcement tool is appropriate, it will be used. If it is not, it will be ignored. Thus, if customary procedures are commonly used as a means of resolving disputes or punishing those who transgress, it is entirely reasonable (and appropriate), in our view to use such measures to enforce the provisions of a modern land development law. Indeed, the use of such measures may render such a law more "modern" than one which imports westernized enforcement tools that are simply inappropriate to the circumstances at hand.

CHAPTER IX - REVENUE POLICY AND LAND USE PLANNING

The issue of revenue is relevant to the land development process in at least two respects. On the one hand, money is an essential ingredient in realizing the development activities which are proposed by a development plan. Obviously, irrigation laterals are not built, seeds are not sown and forests are not maintained unless someone foots the bill. Similarly it is revenue which drives the development process itself. Personnel, data collection and processing, vehicles, offices and office equipment all cost money and, in a developing country, money is frequently a scarce commodity.

Somewhat paradoxically, however, while revenue is critical to the land use planning process, legislation which establishes and guides the working of that process rarely refers to the revenue expenditures necessary for the process to operate. Indeed, apart from scattered references to the collection of permit and license fees or the imposition of criminal or civil fines, none of the legislation cited in this work commits government to a particular level of funding.

The reasons for this reluctance to make direct reference to funding are several, we think, and are not necessarily limited to the circumstances found in developing countries. First, of course, is the difficulty of determining the level of expenditure to be specified. Administrative duties change, the rate of inflation increases or declines and, as a result, it becomes pointless to specify funding at a level which begs for amendment after only a few months. Second, it is usual in many countries for revenue matters to be dealt with collectively in revenue legislation - for instance a budget bill - which permits legislators, ministers and others to compare expenditures and make trade-offs between and among competing government programmes. Creating government revenue obligations and specifying revenue sources in a variety of substantive laws would tend to fragment this process and could well leave government scratching its collective head in wonder about how public revenues are being spent. Moreover, piecing together the budget is often a task alloted to a minister of finance who probably would oppose legislative efforts to specify revenue levels and sources and thus dilute his own authority over such matters.

Finally, there also seems to be a less definable reluctance on the part of political officials to statutorily guarantee the funding of government programmes. Perhaps this reluctance is connected with political control; an agency or programme with a legal guarantee of revenue may, after all, be less flexible when it is asked to bend to the wishes of high level elected or appointed officials. Perhaps too, there is a fear that a financially independent agency or programme may be less accountable to its own statutory mandate. Whatever the cause, this more amorphous opposition to a revenue guarantee will likely contribute to a rejection of any effort to orient land use legislation toward revenue provisions.

Does this mean then that the lawyer or planner should be unconcerned with revenue matters ? Clearly not. Even if proposed land development legislation does not deal directly with the subject of funding for the operation of a land use planning mechanism, it is highly important to study the government's revenue policy as it relates to land use. It is important because such policy has considerable bearing upon the question of who, in fact, will control the land use development process. More specifically, the revenue policy issue may significantly influence the participation or exclusion of different levels of government in the land use planning process. Two examples serve to illustrate : Nepal, where tax revenues are raised and spent at the local level for development,and the Sudan, where the policy has been to restrict local revenue sources.

In Nepal, the Decentralization act of 1982 provides for formulation of development financing at the local level. Each village Panchayat (people's council) for example, is directed to request the appropriate higher level District Panchayat to levy a "Panchayat Development and Land Tax" in the village area [172/]. Prior to making such a request, the village Panchayat or Council is required to have prepared : 1) a plan indicating where the tax income will be spent; 2) a "rough estimate" of the cost of its proposed development programme; and 3) how the total plan of development is to be financed and how much of that financing comes from the Panchayat Development and Land Tax [173/].

Upon receiving such a request, and after its own investigation, the District Panchayat requests the central government to levy a development and land tax whose revenue yield is then split between the local Panchayat, the District Panchayat and the national government in the proportion of 85-10-5 [174/]. In addition, the law provides that in the event of a default in payment of the tax (by local landowners) the District level government shall "realize" the amount of the tax as "Government dues" [175/]. Although the law does not define the term "realize", it suggests, nonetheless, that the government supports the local revenue raising effort.

By way of contrast, the policy of the Sudan appears to be one of retaining revenue control exclusively at the central level of government. The Regional Government Act of 1981, for example, restricts regional government revenues to monies obtained from regional projects and certain limited direct and indirect taxes, and then expressly prohibits regional levies on a laundry-list of sources, including : imports and exports; capital profits; commercial dealings

---

172/ Nepal Decentralization Act (1982), Sec. 20.

173/ *Ibid.*

174/ *Ibid.*, Secs. 20(2), 20(4).

175/ *Ibid.*, Sec. 22.

or investments; and inter-regional goods and services 176/. Revenues for local government in the Sudan are even more restricted and are limited by the People's Local Government Act of 1971 to fees and duties imposed on the limited range of services which are performed by Local District Councils 177/.

As exemplified by Nepal and the Sudan, the differences in government revenue policy can have an enormous impact upon the process of land-use planning. A government whose revenue policy favors the national government will likely be more inclined to favor a centralized land use planning infrastructure. Indeed, in the absence of special local revenue collection measures, a decentralized planning process might well atrophy for lack of operating revenue. On the other hand, a government which favors decentralized decision-making and backs up its preference with a revenue policy that involves revenue sharing at all levels is more likely to be receptive to land use legislation which provides for a planning and implementation infrastructure whose focus is local. Such a localized infrastructure is, in turn, more likely to work, because there may be more local revenue available.

This is not to say, of course, that a government whose revenue policy favors centralization will necessarily be opposed to land-use planning legislation which emphasizes decision-making at the local level; nor that a government whose revenue policy favors local government will necessarily oppose centralized land use planning. It is to suggest, however, that such legislative proposals do cut against prevailing revenue policy and that the lawyer or planner who understands this fact will be better able to devise a functioning planning structure than one who proceeds ahead in ignorance of these sometimes subtle government preferences.

176/ See Wilkinson and Christy, review of Agricultural Legislation in Sudan, TCP/SUD/2210, FAO, 1983.

177/ *Ibid.*

Nor is the importance of revenue control limited only to monies which are generated inside the country; for many developing countries, the ability to influence the expenditures of international aid funds translates to substantial influence over the country's economic development. Thus, for example the Minister of Finance may have a limited role to play in connection with the development of land use plans or the formulation of development projects. If, however, it is the Minister of Finance who has the authority to deal with aid donors and if it is the Minister of Finance through whom international development funds are channeled, then it is a safe bet that the Minister of Finance, in fact, will have a major role to play in the land development process. Accordingly, in such circumstances, it would be appropriate to consider bringing the Ministry of Finance into the development process at an early stage, perhaps even as a member of the group which develops the country's global land use plan or approves plans developed at the sub-national level. Not only would this serve to acquaint the Ministry with the technical, social and environmental issues that pertain to land use development in general and to specific projects in particular, it would also give the Ministry a stake in seeing that the plans which it has helped to prepare are, in fact, implemented as proposed.

Finally, and apart from the matter of using revenue control to influence the development process, we believe it is important to give thought to the matter of development incentives. Liberal allowances for the repatriation of profits as well as tax holidays are frequently used by countries seeking development as a means to attract outside investment. They may conceivably form part of a development plan which seeks to channel investment into a particular region by making investment there comparatively more attractive to investors than investment elsewhere within the country.

In general terms, we have no criticism to voice with respect to the use of such concessions or incentives. As with all such concessions, the potential for abuse exists and it would be time well spent if a brief investigation were made of the situation in the country at hand. Conceivably, of course, there may already be an investment code or other legislation which deals with such matters in detail. On the other hand, there may be no extant legislation which imposes limits on the kind or extent of concessions which can be made. In these circumstances there would appear to be considerable utility in investigating whether concession abuses have occurred in connection with land development, whether government officials have any thoughts about how to stop such abuses in the future and whether the mandate to develop land use legislation extends to the incorporation of controls on the extension of tax and profits concessions. If such an investigation produces affirmative answers to these questions, then we believe it would be worthwhile consulting some of the relatively extensive literature which has been developed in connection with proposed codes of conduct concerning the behavior of multi-national corporations [178/].

178/ See, for example, the "Declaration of OECD Member Government on International Investment and Multi-National Enterprises" OECD, Paris 21 June 1976, which *inter alia* proposes disallowance of some undesirable activities of firms, including unfair transfer pricing and improper payments (i.e., bribes); the "Code of Conduct for Transnational Enterprises", Sistema Econónomico Latinoamerican (SELA), 5 January 1977, which provides, *inter alia*, that multi-nationals "shall conduct their operations in a manner that results in net receipt of financial resources for the host country" (Point 8); U.N. Conference on Trade and Development (UNCTAD), "An International Code of Conduct on the Transfer of Technology", 12 May 1981, Annex I, pages 1014 which, among other things, sets forth a Set of Principles and Rules dealing with abusive intra-corporate practices. See also Brasick, "U.N. Control of Restrictive Business Practices", 17 Journal of World Trade Law, No. 4, p. 337 and Crosse, "Codes of Conduct for Multi-National Enterprises", 16 Journal of World Trade Law, No. 5, p. 414.

CHAPTER X - A LEGAL STRUCTURE FOR MAKING LAND USE DECISIONS

In this final chapter we discuss one proposed legislative approach to the problems of land-use decision making in developing countries [179/]. Not surpringly perhaps, our proposal follows the recommendations set forth in the preceding chapters of this work.

We would begin our drafting with the basics. After determining (or even formulating) the government's policies, priorities and objectives regarding the use of rural land, we would state them clearly in language that leaves as little room as possible for disagreement about the purposes which the law is intended to serve. In essence this means a statement of purposes which is more, rather than less, detailed. Because specifics are generally harder to draft than platitudes - and also are likely to provoke more controversy - this likely means a longer and more combative drafting effort. It is, however, an effort that is worthwhile in our view since a more specific statement of purposes will : 1) provide clearer direction to the individuals who implement the law, 2) allow less room for manoeuvre by those seeking to protect or advance an interest by means that conflict with the law's intent and 3) serve as a clearer standard against which the capability of the decision makers and the legality of their decisions can be measured. In short, the extra effort required to draft a more detailed statement of purposes will be repaid in a more certain - and thus effective - law.

After drafting the purposes which the proposed law is intended to serve, we would examine the ways in which government and land users currently make decisions about the use of land. In essence this means examining existing government decision making structures - both formal and informal - as well as prevailing customary practices. Moreover, because people seem to adapt better

---

179/ There are, of course, a variety of legislative approaches which may improve the way in which decisions about the use of land are made. In presenting the approach set forth herein, we should not be viewed as attempting to pre-empt any other legislative proposals.

to systems which are familiar and comfortable, we would orient this examination of existing decision-making structures in a way that asks first whether an existing system works - in whole or in part - and whether it is possible to formalize the working parts through legislation. Only if it is found that existing systems (including customary practices) do not work to produce national land use decisions or cannot be made to work through legislative attention, would we resort to the creation of an entirely new decision-making structure.

In attempting to determine whether an existing system "works" to produce "rational" land use decisions, there are several factors to which we would pay especially close attention. First, we would examine whether land use decisions are grounded upon some kind of data base and, if so, of what sort. In pursuing this point, we would assess whether decisions are made in light of the kinds of data elements described above in Chapter V. As noted previously, those elements represent a kind of minimum data level without which it would be difficult to make technically sound land use decisions.

Second, in determining whether an existing system "works" to produce rational land use decisions, we would attempt to determine how the system functions in building a consensus about land use. More particularly we would look to see how the system horizontally and vertically integrates the views of those interested in decisions about land. On the one hand this means investigating the extent to which the system achieves a multi-disciplinary approach to decision making that includes not just development interests, but also social, health and environmental concerns in the decision-making process (horizontal integration). On the other hand, this means examining how successfully the system incorporates the views of persons from different levels (local, district or regional, for example) into the decision-making process. If, for example, it is found that decisions are made by fiat from a central government bureau located a great distance from the land in question, our suspicion would be that the system doesn't work - unless of course there is an exceedingly strong enforcement mechanism. If, instead, there is public involvement in the existing system - particularly at the land user level - the chance that the existing system will actually achieve the land uses which are decided upon at the policy level, substantially improves.

The mention of different levels of decision-making suggests another element which, in our view, should be part of any examination of the functioning of any existing land use decision-making structure; viz, the matter of scale. If the existing structure produces only global plans for land use (for instance a general 5 year plan of economic development) or only locally made land use decisions (for instance, by the landowner who decides what crop he will plant without reference to any plan) our guess is that nor much real land use "planning" takes place. If on the other hand, an existing system produces both global and local decisions and - importantly - links those decisions, then it is more likely that the system produces rational, planned results.

Finally, in the course of examining an existing system of land decision making, we would look at the means by which decisions are implemented. In pursuing this investigation, we would use the description of implementation measures laid out in Chapter VII above, as a guide in asking, for example, does the system provide for the zoning of land in accordance with a land use plan ? Or does it provide for the issuance of development permits or the acquisition of land to fulfill development objectives ?

The foregoing checklist of consideration to be examined when evaluating an existing system of land use decision-making also serves as a framework for legislative drafting if it is found that there is no existing system or that the system which exists fails to produce "rational" results. For instance, the issue of scale suggests that provision should be made first for the development of a global or national plan which gives government the opportunity to determine overall national objectives and, through development of a very large scale map, make rough determinations (probably region-by-region, and perhaps district-by-district if a smaller scale is used) of the uses to which rural land should be devoted in order to achieve national objectives.

Because a global plan is unlikely to be on a small enough scale to allow the detailed planning necessary for implementation of the government's goals, the law should also prescribe the development of site specific plans (see Chapter V) at the regional or district level. To ensure consistency with national objectives the law should provide as well for review of such regional or district plans by a higher level authority closer to national objectives.

The issue of consensus also bears upon the drafting of legislation. The development of a consensus through the horizontal integration of different land use perspectives suggests that global and regional plans should each be developed by a multi-disciplinary group reflecting a spectrum of interests. In practice this may mean including persons who represent not only governement agricultural development interests, but also health, environment, financial, and social interests. Among agricultural interests it may mean the inclusion not only of irrigaton or mechanised farming interests, but also of officials who represent forestry and fishery concerns as well as those who represent pastoralists and shifting cultivators. Finally, it may mean including land users themselves through representatives from farmer organizations or cooperatives [180/].

The issue of vertical integration is also of import to the legislative drafter. In order to link regional or district plans to the larger scale global planning effort it is useful, we believe, to provide for vertical cross-pollinization by including one or more regional or district

---

180/ The exact composition of the planning body at each level will, of course, vary from case to case thus making it impossible to specify a standard membership list here. Fair warning should be made, however, that the membership of any high level policy making body is a politically charged question. From experience, it is our guess that the legislative drafter will be forced by circumstances to spend more time on the legal provisions relating to such membership than on any other part of the proposed legislation. Nor unfortunately, can this task reasonably be avoided. It is important, in our view, to nail down membership as precisely as possible. Leaving the matter open may tend to result in a membership unduly biased in favor of or against a particular interest group.

representatives within the global planning group authorized by the land use statute being drafted. The linkage between a global land use plan and smaller scale regional or district plans would also be strengthened by providing for review and, if necessary, for modification of the smaller scale plans by the global planners to ensure that the more local plan conforms to national policies.

It is also extremely important, in our view, for land use legislation to prescribe at least the minimum data elements necessary for competent land use planning. If those data elements are already being collected and used, such a legislative requirement should impose no additional practical burden upon the country's land use officials. If, on the other hand, the minimum necessary data elements are not being collected and used, such legislation will provide the legal impetus for doing so.

The review of existing implementation measures should reveal the deficiencies which exist in any current land use decision system and thus provide the basis for drafting implementation measures in a new law. Insofar as implementing provisions are concerned, our preference is to keep things simple. It doesn't do much good, for example, to legislatively erect an elaborate permit system with applications, hearings and review procedures in a country where many people cannot read, have no conception of a formal appeal and have limited means of attending a hearing in any event. In such circumstances, successful implementation may depend upon the building of a consensus at local levels, with implementation left in the hands of village or tribal leaders. On the other hand, where there exists a higher level of education and a better infrastructure, somewhat more sophisticated implementation measures may succeed. The description of implementation measures set forth in Chapter VII above, serves to indicate the kinds of proposals which could be written into a land use law in such circumstances.

Apart from setting forth basic purposes, creating basic infrastructure, tackling the issue of scale and prescribing measures of implementation, there are several additional useful functions which competently drafted land use legislation can serve. Of great importance, in our view, is the possibility of guiding land use decision-makers in actually making choices from among competing land use alternatives. Initially, the legislation can lead decision-makers at any level through the steps necessary to reach a determination of land use requirements and land characteristics (see Chapter V). Once a series of land use alternatives has been derived through the matching of requirements with characteristics, the legislation can then assist planners in making the choice by laying out the principles which must be observed in choosing a reccommended use. One group of suggested land use principles has already been described above in Chapter VI. Undoubtedly the drafter faced with the real-life problems encountered in every developing country will make significant amendments and additions to this list. The point, however, is that considerable utility will be derived from including some grouping of decision-making principles in the proposed land use law.

Additional benefit will aso be provided, we believe, through the inclusion of legal provisions relating to the monitoring and enforcement of land use decisions. As we have noted heretofore in Chapter VIII, the legal drafter is unlikely to find much local legislation dealing with either subject in any depth. Well considered monitoring and enforcement provisions, however, are of considerable importance to the successful functioning of any system of land use decision-making - as we have explained above. Thus, we would conclude our proposed law with monitoring and enforcement language tailored as closely as possible to the practical circumstances which exist in the country involved.

For those who find schematic outlines helpful, our drafting effort would be depicted roughly as follows :

STATEMENT OF PURPOSE(S)

INFRASTRUCTURE

National

1. Membership: multi-disciplinary (horizontal or vertical)

2. Function:
   a) collect and evaluate data relevant to global planning
      (1) cadastral survey
      (2) thematic maps
      (3) climatic data
      (4) soils survey data
      (5) hydrologic survey data

   b) use data to generate:
      (1) land use requirements
      (2) land characteristics to yield:
      (3) resultant global land use alternatives

   c) prepare global plan by selecting from among global land use alternatives in accordance with land use principles

   d) guide and review district and regional plans

District or Regional

1. Membership: multi-disciplinary (horizontal or vertical)

2. Function:
   a) collect and evaluate data relevant to district or regional plans :
      (1) district or regional cadastral survey
      (2) thematic maps
      (3) district or regional climatic data
      (4) district or regional soils data

   b) use data to generate:
      (1) district or regional land use requirements
      (2) district or regional land characteristics to yield:
      (3) resultant site specific land use alternatives

   c) prepare site specific district or regional plan by selecting from district or regional site specific alternatives in accordance with land use principles

   d) monitor and enforce district and regional site specific plans

Planning Principles

1. Benefits and direct and secondary costs to be considered
2. No implementation unless benefits of an alternative exceed its direct and secondary costs
3. Where two or more alternatives justified, the alternative which has lower social and environmental costs to be preferred
4. Any proposed land use to be reasonable in the circumstances
5. No person poses an unalterable right to a particular land use and government may alter or modify any use when the public interest requires
6. Other land use planning principles

Implementation Measures

1. Legal Implementation Measures
   a) Development Permits and Orders
   b) Zoning Classifications
   c) Public Trust Authority
   d) Acquisition of Ownership Interest
2. Extra-Legal Implementation Measures
   a) Extesnion Services
   b) Training
   c) Government Pricing Policy

Monitoring and Enforcement

1. Monitoring
   a) a clearly stated reason for monitoring
   b) a practical monitoring mechanism
   c) a monitoring process which is consistent
   d) unequivocal right of access for monitoring purposes
   2. Enforcement.

While the foregoing scheme need not be followed slavishly, we do nonetheless believe it contains all of the basic elements necessary for a land use decision-making system that will work to produce "rational" results. And that, after all, is the bottom line measure of the utility of any planning process.